THE MESSAGE OF PSALMS

THE MESSAGE® OF PSALMS

IN CONTEMPORARY LANGUAGE

EUGENE H. PETERSON

A NavPress resource published in alliance with Tyndale House Publishers, Inc.

NavPress is the publishing ministry of The Navigators, an international Christian organization and leader in personal spiritual development. NavPress is committed to helping people grow spiritually and enjoy lives of meaning and hope through personal and group resources that are biblically rooted, culturally relevant, and highly practical.

For more information, visit www.NavPress.com.

Cover design by Dean H. Renninger

A NavPress resource published in alliance with Tyndale House Publishers, Inc.

ISBN 978-1-61747-273-2

Published in association with Alive Literary Agency, Inc., 7680 Goddard St., Suite 200, Colorado Springs, CO 80920. www.aliveliterary.com

Printed in the United States of America

24 23 22 21 20 19 18
11 10 9 8 7 6 5

INTRODUCTION

PSALMS

Most Christians for most of the Christian centuries have learned to pray by praying the Psalms. The Hebrews, with several centuries of a head start on us in matters of prayer and worship, provided us with this prayer book that gives us a language adequate for responding to the God who speaks to us.

The stimulus to paraphrase the Psalms into a contemporary idiom comes from my lifetime of work as a pastor. As a pastor I was charged with, among other things, teaching people to pray, helping them to give voice to the entire experience of being human, and to do it both honestly and thoroughly. I found that it was not as easy as I expected. Getting started is easy enough. The impulse to pray is deep within us, at the very center of our created being, and so practically anything will do to get us started—"Help" and "Thanks!" are our basic prayers. But honesty and thoroughness don't come quite as spontaneously.

Faced with the prospect of conversation with a holy God who speaks worlds into being, it is not surprising that we have trouble. We feel awkward and out of place: "I'm not good enough for this. I'll wait until I clean up my act and prove that I am a decent person." Or we excuse ourselves on the grounds that our vocabulary is inadequate: "Give me a few months—or years!—to practice prayers that are polished enough for such a sacred meeting. Then I won't feel so stuttery and ill at ease."

My usual response when presented with these difficulties is to put the Psalms in a person's hand and say, "Go home and pray these. You've got wrong ideas about prayer; the praying you find in these Psalms will dispel the wrong ideas and introduce you to the real thing." A common response of those who do what I ask is surprise—they don't expect this kind of thing in the Bible. And then I express surprise at their surprise: "Did you think these would be the prayers of *nice* people? Did you think the psalmists' language would be polished and polite?"

Untutored, we tend to think that prayer is what good people do when they are doing their best. It is not. Inexperienced, we suppose that there must be an "insider" language that must be acquired before God takes us seriously in our prayer. There is not. Prayer is elemental, not advanced, language. It is the means by which our language becomes honest, true, and personal in response to God. It is the means by which we get everything in our lives out in the open before God.

But even with the Psalms in their hands and my pastoral encouragement, people often tell me that they still don't get it. In English translation, the Psalms often sound smooth and polished, sonorous with Elizabethan rhythms and diction. As literature, they are beyond compare. But as *prayer*, as the utterances of men and women passionate for God in moments of anger and praise and lament, these translations miss something. *Grammatically*, they are accurate. The scholarship undergirding the translations is superb and devout. But as *prayers* they are not quite right. The Psalms in Hebrew are earthy and rough. They are not genteel. They are not the prayers of nice people, couched in cultured language.

And so in my pastoral work of teaching people to

pray, I started paraphrasing the Psalms into the rhythms and idiom of contemporary English. I wanted to provide men and women access to the immense range and the terrific energies of prayer in the kind of language that is most immediate to them, which also happens to be the language in which these psalm prayers were first expressed and written by David and his successors.

I continue to want to do that, convinced that only as we develop raw honesty and detailed thoroughness in our praying do we become whole, truly human in Jesus Christ, who also prayed the Psalms.

PSALMS

1

How well God must like you—
    you don't walk in the ruts of those blind-as-bats,
    you don't stand with the good-for-nothings,
    you don't take your seat among the know-it-alls.

Instead you thrill to GOD's Word,
    you chew on Scripture day and night.
You're a tree replanted in Eden,
    bearing fresh fruit every month,
Never dropping a leaf,
    always in blossom.

You're not at all like the wicked,
    who are mere windblown dust—
Without defense in court,
    unfit company for innocent people.

GOD charts the road you take.
The road *they* take leads to nowhere.

2

Why the big noise, nations?
Why the mean plots, peoples?
Earth-leaders push for position,
Demagogues and delegates meet for summit talks,
The God-deniers, the Messiah-defiers:
"Let's get free of God!

Cast loose from Messiah!"
Heaven-throned God breaks out laughing.
At first he's amused at their presumption;
Then he gets good and angry.
Furiously, he shuts them up:
"Don't you know there's a King in Zion? A
coronation banquet
Is spread for him on the holy summit."

Let me tell you what GOD said next.
He said, "You're my son,
And today is your birthday.
What do you want? Name it:
Nations as a present? continents as a prize?
You can command them all to dance for you,
Or throw them out with tomorrow's trash."

So, rebel-kings, use your heads;
Upstart-judges, learn your lesson:
Worship GOD in adoring embrace,
Celebrate in trembling awe. Kiss Messiah!
Your very lives are in danger, you know;
His anger is about to explode,
But if you make a run for God—you won't regret it!

3

A David psalm, when he escaped for his life from Absalom, his son

GOD! Look! Enemies past counting!
Enemies sprouting like mushrooms,

Mobs of them all around me, roaring their mockery:
"Hah! No help for *him* from God!"

But you, GOD, shield me on all sides;
You ground my feet, you lift my head high;
With all my might I shout up to GOD,
His answers thunder from the holy mountain.

I stretch myself out. I sleep.
Then I'm up again—rested, tall and steady,
Fearless before the enemy mobs
Coming at me from all sides.

Up, GOD! My God, help me!
Slap their faces,
First this cheek, then the other,
Your fist hard in their teeth!

Real help comes from GOD.
Your blessing clothes your people!

4

A David psalm

When I call, give me answers. God, take my side!
Once, in a tight place, you gave me room;
Now I'm in trouble again: grace me! hear me!

You rabble—how long do I put up with your scorn?
How long will you lust after lies?
How long will you live crazed by illusion?

Look at this: look
Who got picked by GOD!
He listens the split second I call to him.

Complain if you must, but don't lash out.
Keep your mouth shut, and let your heart do the
talking.
Build your case before God and wait for his verdict.

Why is everyone hungry for *more*? "More, more,"
they say.
"More, more."
I have God's more-than-enough,
More joy in one ordinary day

Than they get in all their shopping sprees.
At day's end I'm ready for sound sleep,
For you, GOD, have put my life back together.

5

A David psalm

Listen, GOD! Please, pay attention!
Can you make sense of these ramblings,
my groans and cries?
King-God, I need your help.
Every morning
you'll hear me at it again.
Every morning
I lay out the pieces of my life

on your altar
and watch for fire to descend.

You don't socialize with Wicked,
or invite Evil over as your houseguest.
Hot-Air-Boaster collapses in front of you;
you shake your head over Mischief-Maker.
GOD destroys Lie-Speaker;
Blood-Thirsty and Truth-Bender disgust you.

And here I am, your invited guest—
it's incredible!
I enter your house; here I am,
prostrate in your inner sanctum,
Waiting for directions
to get me safely through enemy lines.

Every word they speak is a land mine;
their lungs breathe out poison gas.
Their throats are gaping graves,
their tongues slick as mudslides.
Pile on the guilt, God!
Let their so-called wisdom wreck them.
Kick them out! They've had their chance.

But you'll welcome us with open arms
when we run for cover to you.
Let the party last all night!
Stand guard over our celebration.
You are famous, GOD, for welcoming God-seekers,
for decking us out in delight.

6

A David psalm

Please, GOD, no more yelling,
no more trips to the woodshed.
Treat me nice for a change;
I'm so starved for affection.

Can't you see I'm black and blue,
beaten up badly in bones and soul?
GOD, how long will it take
for you to let up?

Break in, GOD, and break up this fight;
if you love me at all, get me out of here.
I'm no good to you dead, am I?
I can't sing in your choir if I'm buried in some tomb!

I'm tired of all this—so tired. My bed
has been floating forty days and nights
On the flood of my tears.
My mattress is soaked, soggy with tears.
The sockets of my eyes are black holes;
nearly blind, I squint and grope.

Get out of here, you Devil's crew:
at last GOD has heard my sobs.
My requests have all been granted,
my prayers are answered.

Cowards, my enemies disappear.
Disgraced, they turn tail and run.

7

A David psalm

God! God! I am running to you for dear life;
the chase is wild.
If they catch me, I'm finished:
ripped to shreds by foes fierce as lions,
dragged into the forest and left
unlooked for, unremembered.

God, if I've done what they say—
betrayed my friends,
ripped off my enemies—
If my hands are really that dirty,
let them get me, walk all over me,
leave me flat on my face in the dirt.

Stand up, God; pit your holy fury
against my furious enemies.
Wake up, God. My accusers have packed
the courtroom; it's judgment time.
Take your place on the bench, reach for your gavel,
throw out the false charges against me.
I'm ready, confident in your verdict:
"Innocent."

Close the book on Evil, God,
but publish your mandate for us.

You get us ready for life:
you probe for our soft spots,
you knock off our rough edges.
And I'm feeling so fit, so safe:
made right, kept right.
God in solemn honor does things right,
but his nerves are sandpapered raw.

Nobody gets by with anything.
God is already in action—
Sword honed on his whetstone,
bow strung, arrow on the string,
Lethal weapons in hand,
each arrow a flaming missile.

Look at that guy!
He had sex with sin,
he's pregnant with evil.
Oh, look! He's having
the baby—a Lie-Baby!

See that man shoveling day after day,
digging, then concealing, his man-trap
down that lonely stretch of road?
Go back and look again—you'll see him in it
headfirst,
legs waving in the breeze.
That's what happens:
mischief backfires;
violence boomerangs.

I'm thanking God, who makes things right.
I'm singing the fame of heaven-high God.

8

A David psalm

God, brilliant Lord,
    yours is a household name.

Nursing infants gurgle choruses about you;
    toddlers shout the songs
That drown out enemy talk,
    and silence atheist babble.

I look up at your macro-skies, dark and enormous,
    your handmade sky-jewelry,
Moon and stars mounted in their settings.
    Then I look at my micro-self and wonder,
Why do you bother with us?
    Why take a second look our way?

Yet we've so narrowly missed being gods,
    bright with Eden's dawn light.
You put us in charge of your handcrafted world,
    repeated to us your Genesis-charge,
Made us stewards of sheep and cattle,
    even animals out in the wild,
Birds flying and fish swimming,
    whales singing in the ocean deeps.

GOD, brilliant Lord,
your name echoes around the world.

9

A David psalm

I'm thanking you, GOD, from a full heart,
I'm writing the book on your wonders.
I'm whistling, laughing, and jumping for joy;
I'm singing your song, High God.

The day my enemies turned tail and ran,
they stumbled on you and fell on their faces.
You took over and set everything right;
when I needed you, you were there, taking charge.

You blow the whistle on godless nations;
you throw dirty players out of the game,
wipe their names right off the roster.
Enemies disappear from the sidelines,
their reputation trashed,
their names erased from the halls of fame.

GOD holds the high center,
he sees and sets the world's mess right.
He decides what is right for us earthlings,
gives people their just deserts.

GOD's a safe-house for the battered,
a sanctuary during bad times.

The moment you arrive, you relax;
    you're never sorry you knocked.

Sing your songs to Zion-dwelling God,
    tell his stories to everyone you meet:
How he tracks down killers
    yet keeps his eye on us,
    registers every whimper and moan.

Be kind to me, God;
    I've been kicked around long enough.
Once you've pulled me back
    from the gates of death,
I'll write the book on Hallelujahs;
    on the corner of Main and First
    I'll hold a street meeting;
I'll be the song leader; we'll fill the air
    with salvation songs.

They're trapped, those godless countries,
    in the very snares they set,
Their feet all tangled
    in the net they spread.
They have no excuse;
    the way God works is well-known.
The shrewd machinery made by the wicked
    has maimed their own hands.

The wicked bought a one-way
    ticket to hell.

No longer will the poor be nameless—
no more humiliation for the humble.
Up, GOD! Aren't you fed up with their empty
strutting?
Expose these grand pretensions!
Shake them up, GOD!
Show them how silly they look.

10

GOD, are you avoiding me?
Where are you when I need you?
Full of hot air, the wicked
are hot on the trail of the poor.
Trip them up, tangle them up
in their fine-tuned plots.

The wicked are windbags,
the swindlers have foul breath.
The wicked snub GOD,
their noses stuck high in the air.
Their graffiti are scrawled on the walls:
"Catch us if you can!" "God is dead."

They care nothing for what you think;
if you get in their way, they blow you off.
They live (they think) a charmed life:
"We can't go wrong. This is our lucky year!"

They carry a mouthful of spells,
their tongues spit venom like adders.

They hide behind ordinary people,
    then pounce on their victims.

They mark the luckless,
    then wait like a hunter in a blind;
When the poor wretch wanders too close,
    they stab him in the back.

The hapless fool is kicked to the ground,
    the unlucky victim is brutally axed.
He thinks God has dumped him,
    he's sure that God is indifferent to his plight.

Time to get up, GOD—get moving.
    The luckless think they're Godforsaken.
They wonder why the wicked scorn God
    and get away with it,
Why the wicked are so cocksure
    they'll never come up for audit.

But you know all about it—
    the contempt, the abuse.
I dare to believe that the luckless
    will get lucky someday in you.
You won't let them down:
    orphans won't be orphans forever.

Break the wicked right arms,
    break all the evil left arms.
Search and destroy
    every sign of crime.

GOD's grace and order wins;
godlessness loses.

The victim's faint pulse picks up;
the hearts of the hopeless pump red blood
as you put your ear to their lips.
Orphans get parents,
the homeless get homes.
The reign of terror is over,
the rule of the gang lords is ended.

11

A David psalm

I've already run for dear life
straight to the arms of GOD.
So why would I run away now
when you say,

"Run to the mountains; the evil
bows are bent, the wicked arrows
Aimed to shoot under cover of darkness
at every heart open to God.
The bottom's dropped out of the country;
good people don't have a chance"?

But GOD hasn't moved to the mountains;
his holy address hasn't changed.
He's in charge, as always, his eyes
taking everything in, his eyelids

Unblinking, examining Adam's flesh and blood
inside and out, not missing a thing.
He tests the good and the bad alike;
if anyone cheats, God's outraged.
Fail the test and you're out,
out in a hail of firestones,
Drinking from a canteen
filled with hot desert wind.

God's business is putting things right;
he loves getting the lines straight,
Setting us straight. Once we're standing tall,
we can look him straight in the eye.

12

A David psalm

Quick, God, I need your helping hand!
The last decent person just went down,
All the friends I depended on gone.
Everyone talks in lie language;
Lies slide off their oily lips.
They doubletalk with forked tongues.

Slice their lips off their faces! Pull
The braggart tongues from their mouths!
I'm tired of hearing, "We can talk anyone into
anything!
Our lips manage the world."

Into the hovels of the poor,
Into the dark streets where the homeless groan,
God speaks:
"I've had enough; I'm on my way
To heal the ache in the heart of the wretched."

God's words are pure words,
Pure silver words refined seven times
In the fires of his word-kiln,
Pure on earth as well as in heaven.
GOD, keep us safe from their lies,
From the wicked who stalk us with lies,
From the wicked who collect honors
For their wonderful lies.

13

A David psalm

Long enough, GOD—
you've ignored me long enough.
I've looked at the back of your head
long enough. Long enough
I've carried this ton of trouble,
lived with a stomach full of pain.
Long enough my arrogant enemies
have looked down their noses at me.

Take a good look at me, GOD, my God;
I want to look life in the eye,

So no enemy can get the best of me
or laugh when I fall on my face.

I've thrown myself headlong into your arms—
I'm celebrating your rescue.
I'm singing at the top of my lungs,
I'm so full of answered prayers.

14

A David psalm

Bilious and bloated, they gas,
"God is gone."
Their words are poison gas,
fouling the air; they poison
Rivers and skies;
thistles are their cash crop.

GOD sticks his head out of heaven.
He looks around.
He's looking for someone not stupid—
one man, even, God-expectant,
just one God-ready woman.

He comes up empty. A string
of zeros. Useless, unshepherded
Sheep, taking turns pretending
to be Shepherd.
The ninety and nine
follow their fellow.

Don't they know anything,
    all these predators?
Don't they know
    they can't get away with this—
Treating people like a fast-food meal
    over which they're too busy to pray?

Night is coming for them, and nightmares,
    for God takes the side of victims.
Do you think you can mess
    with the dreams of the poor?
You can't, for God
    makes their dreams come true.

Is there anyone around to save Israel?
    Yes. God is around; God turns life around.
Turned-around Jacob skips rope,
    turned-around Israel sings laughter.

15

A David psalm

God, who gets invited
to dinner at your place?
How do we get on your guest list?

"Walk straight,
    act right,
        tell the truth.

"Don't hurt your friend,
don't blame your neighbor;
despise the despicable.

"Keep your word even when it costs you,
make an honest living,
never take a bribe.

"You'll never get
blacklisted
if you live like this."

16

A David song

Keep me safe, O God,
I've run for dear life to you.
I say to GOD, "Be my Lord!"
Without you, nothing makes sense.

And these God-chosen lives all around—
what splendid friends they make!

Don't just go shopping for a god.
Gods are not for sale.
I swear I'll never treat god-names
like brand-names.

My choice is you, GOD, first and only.
And now I find I'm *your* choice!

You set me up with a house and yard.
    And then you made me your heir!

The wise counsel GOD gives when I'm awake
    is confirmed by my sleeping heart.
Day and night I'll stick with GOD;
    I've got a good thing going and I'm not letting go.

I'm happy from the inside out,
    and from the outside in, I'm firmly formed.
You canceled my ticket to hell—
    that's not my destination!

Now you've got my feet on the life path,
    all radiant from the shining of your face.
Ever since you took my hand,
    I'm on the right way.

17

A David prayer

Listen while I build my case, GOD,
    the most honest prayer you'll ever hear.
Show the world I'm innocent—
    in your heart you know I am.

Go ahead, examine me from inside out,
    surprise me in the middle of the night—
You'll find I'm just what I say I am.
    My words don't run loose.

I'm not trying to get my way
    in the world's way.
I'm trying to get *your* way,
    your Word's way.
I'm staying on your trail;
    I'm putting one foot
In front of the other.
    I'm not giving up.

I call to you, God, because I'm sure of an answer.
    So—answer! bend your ear! listen sharp!
Paint grace-graffiti on the fences;
    take in your frightened children who
Are running from the neighborhood bullies
    straight to you.

Keep your eye on me;
    hide me under your cool wing feathers
From the wicked who are out to get me,
    from mortal enemies closing in.

Their hearts are hard as nails,
    their mouths blast hot air.
They are after me, nipping my heels,
    determined to bring me down,
Lions ready to rip me apart,
    young lions poised to pounce.
Up, GOD: beard them! break them!
    By your sword, free me from their clutches;
Barehanded, GOD, break these mortals,

these flat-earth people who can't think beyond
today.

I'd like to see their bellies
swollen with famine food,
The weeds they've sown
harvested and baked into famine bread,
With second helpings for their children
and crusts for their babies to chew on.

And me? I plan on looking
you full in the face. When I get up,
I'll see your full stature
and live heaven on earth.

18

A David song, which he sang to God after being saved from all his enemies and from Saul

I love you, God—
you make me strong.
God is bedrock under my feet,
the castle in which I live,
my rescuing knight.
My God—the high crag
where I run for dear life,
hiding behind the boulders,
safe in the granite hideout.

I sing to GOD, the Praise-Lofty,
    and find myself safe and saved.

The hangman's noose was tight at my throat;
    devil waters rushed over me.
Hell's ropes cinched me tight;
    death traps barred every exit.

A hostile world! I call to GOD,
    I cry to God to help me.
From his palace he hears my call;
    my cry brings me right into his presence—
    a private audience!

Earth wobbles and lurches;
    huge mountains shake like leaves,
Quake like aspen leaves
    because of his rage.
His nostrils flare, bellowing smoke;
    his mouth spits fire.
Tongues of fire dart in and out;
    he lowers the sky.
He steps down;
    under his feet an abyss opens up.
He's riding a winged creature,
    swift on wind-wings.
Now he's wrapped himself
    in a trenchcoat of black-cloud darkness.
But his cloud-brightness bursts through,
    spraying hailstones and fireballs.

Then God thundered out of heaven;
the High God gave a great shout,
spraying hailstones and fireballs.
God shoots his arrows—pandemonium!
He hurls his lightnings—a rout!
The secret sources of ocean are exposed,
the hidden depths of earth lie uncovered
The moment you roar in protest,
let loose your hurricane anger.

But me he caught—reached all the way
from sky to sea; he pulled me out
Of that ocean of hate, that enemy chaos,
the void in which I was drowning.
They hit me when I was down,
but God stuck by me.
He stood me up on a wide-open field;
I stood there saved—surprised to be loved!

God made my life complete
when I placed all the pieces before him.
When I got my act together,
he gave me a fresh start.
Now I'm alert to God's ways;
I don't take God for granted.
Every day I review the ways he works;
I try not to miss a trick.
I feel put back together,
and I'm watching my step.

GOD rewrote the text of my life
    when I opened the book of my heart to his eyes.

The good people taste your goodness,
The whole people taste your health,
The true people taste your truth,
The bad ones can't figure you out.
You take the side of the down-and-out,
But the stuck-up you take down a notch.

Suddenly, GOD, you floodlight my life;
    I'm blazing with glory, God's glory!
I smash the bands of marauders,
    I vault the highest fences.
What a God! His road
    stretches straight and smooth.
Every GOD-direction is road-tested.
    Everyone who runs toward him
Makes it.

Is there any god like GOD?
    Are we not at bedrock?
Is not this the God who armed me,
    then aimed me in the right direction?
Now I run like a deer;
    I'm king of the mountain.
He shows me how to fight;
    I can bend a bronze bow!
You protect me with salvation-armor;
    you hold me up with a firm hand,

caress me with your gentle ways.
You cleared the ground under me
so my footing was firm.
When I chased my enemies I caught them;
I didn't let go till they were dead men.
I nailed them; they were down for good;
then I walked all over them.
You armed me well for this fight,
you smashed the upstarts.
You made my enemies turn tail,
and I wiped out the haters.
They cried "uncle"
but Uncle didn't come;
They yelled for GOD
and got no for an answer.
I ground them to dust; they gusted in the wind.
I threw them out, like garbage in the gutter.

You rescued me from a squabbling people;
you made me a leader of nations.
People I'd never heard of served me;
the moment they got wind of me they listened.
The foreign devils gave up; they came
on their bellies, crawling from their hideouts.

Live, GOD! Blessings from my Rock,
my free and freeing God, towering!
This God set things right for me
and shut up the people who talked back.

He rescued me from enemy anger,
    he pulled me from the grip of upstarts,
He saved me from the bullies.

That's why I'm thanking you, GOD,
    all over the world.
That's why I'm singing songs
    that rhyme your name.
God's king takes the trophy;
    God's chosen is beloved.
I mean David and all his children—
    always.

19

A David psalm

God's glory is on tour in the skies,
    God-craft on exhibit across the horizon.
Madame Day holds classes every morning,
    Professor Night lectures each evening.

Their words aren't heard,
    their voices aren't recorded,
But their silence fills the earth:
    unspoken truth is spoken everywhere.

God makes a huge dome
    for the sun—a superdome!
The morning sun's a new husband
    leaping from his honeymoon bed,

The daybreaking sun an athlete
racing to the tape.

That's how God's Word vaults across the skies
from sunrise to sunset,
Melting ice, scorching deserts,
warming hearts to faith.

The revelation of God is whole
and pulls our lives together.
The signposts of God are clear
and point out the right road.
The life-maps of God are right,
showing the way to joy.
The directions of God are plain
and easy on the eyes.
God's reputation is twenty-four carat gold,
with a lifetime guarantee.
The decisions of God are accurate
down to the nth degree.

God's Word is better than a diamond,
better than a diamond set between emeralds.
You'll like it better than strawberries in spring,
better than red, ripe strawberries.

There's more: God's Word warns us of danger
and directs us to hidden treasure.
Otherwise how will we find our way?
Or know when we play the fool?

Clean the slate, God, so we can start the day fresh!
    Keep me from stupid sins,
    from thinking I can take over your work;
Then I can start this day sun-washed,
    scrubbed clean of the grime of sin.
These are the words in my mouth;
    these are what I chew on and pray.
Accept them when I place them
    on the morning altar,
O God, my Altar-Rock,
    God, Priest-of-My-Altar.

20

A David psalm

God answer you on the day you crash,
The name God-of-Jacob put you out of harm's reach,
Send reinforcements from Holy Hill,
Dispatch from Zion fresh supplies,
Exclaim over your offerings,
Celebrate your sacrifices,
Give you what your heart desires,
Accomplish your plans.

When you win, we plan to raise the roof
    and lead the parade with our banners.
May all your wishes come true!

That clinches it—help's coming,
an answer's on the way,
everything's going to work out.

See those people polishing their chariots,
and those others grooming their horses?
But we're making garlands for GOD our God.
The chariots will rust,
those horses pull up lame—
and we'll be on our feet, standing tall.

Make the king a winner, GOD;
the day we call, give us your answer.

21

A David psalm

Your strength, GOD, is the king's strength.
Helped, he's hollering Hosannas.
You gave him exactly what he wanted;
you didn't hold back.
You filled his arms with gifts;
you gave him a right royal welcome.
He wanted a good life; you gave it to him,
and then made it a *long* life as a bonus.
You lifted him high and bright as a cumulus cloud,
then dressed him in rainbow colors.
You pile blessings on him;
you make him glad when you smile.

Is it any wonder the king loves GOD?
that he's sticking with the Best?

With a fistful of enemies in one hand
and a fistful of haters in the other,
You radiate with such brilliance
that they cringe as before a furnace.
Now the furnace swallows them whole,
the fire eats them alive!
You purge the earth of their progeny,
you wipe the slate clean.
All their evil schemes, the plots they cook up,
have fizzled—every one.
You sent them packing;
they couldn't face you.

Show your strength, GOD, so no one can miss it.
We are out singing the good news!

22

A David psalm

God, God . . . my God!
Why did you dump me
miles from nowhere?
Doubled up with pain, I call to God
all the day long. No answer. Nothing.
I keep at it all night, tossing and turning.

And you! Are you indifferent, above it all,
    leaning back on the cushions of Israel's praise?
We know you were there for our parents:
    they cried for your help and you gave it;
    they trusted and lived a good life.

And here I am, a nothing—an earthworm,
    something to step on, to squash.
Everyone pokes fun at me;
    they make faces at me, they shake their heads:
"Let's see how GOD handles this one;
    since God likes him so much, let *him* help him!"

And to think you were midwife at my birth,
    setting me at my mother's breasts!
When I left the womb you cradled me;
    since the moment of birth you've been my God.
Then you moved far away
    and trouble moved in next door.
I need a neighbor.

Herds of bulls come at me,
    the raging bulls stampede,
Horns lowered, nostrils flaring,
    like a herd of buffalo on the move.

I'm a bucket kicked over and spilled,
    every joint in my body has been pulled apart.
My heart is a blob
    of melted wax in my gut.

I'm dry as a bone,
my tongue black and swollen.
They have laid me out for burial
in the dirt.

Now packs of wild dogs come at me;
thugs gang up on me.
They pin me down hand and foot,
and lock me in a cage—a bag
Of bones in a cage, stared at
by every passerby.
They take my wallet and the shirt off my back,
and then throw dice for my clothes.

You, GOD—don't put off my rescue!
Hurry and help me!
Don't let them cut my throat;
don't let those mongrels devour me.
If you don't show up soon,
I'm done for—gored by the bulls,
meat for the lions.

Here's the story I'll tell my friends when they come
to worship,
and punctuate it with Hallelujahs:
Shout Hallelujah, you God-worshipers;
give glory, you sons of Jacob;
adore him, you daughters of Israel.
He has never let you down,
never looked the other way

when you were being kicked around.
He has never wandered off to do his own thing;
he has been right there, listening.

Here in this great gathering for worship
I have discovered this praise-life.
And I'll do what I promised right here
in front of the God-worshipers.
Down-and-outers sit at GOD's table
and eat their fill.
Everyone on the hunt for God
is here, praising him.
"Live it up, from head to toe.
Don't ever quit!"

From the four corners of the earth
people are coming to their senses,
are running back to GOD.
Long-lost families
are falling on their faces before him.
GOD has taken charge;
from now on he has the last word.

All the power-mongers are before him
—worshiping!
All the poor and powerless, too
—worshiping!
Along with those who never got it together
—worshiping!

Our children and their children
    will get in on this
As the word is passed along
    from parent to child.
Babies not yet conceived
    will hear the good news—
    that God does what he says.

23

A David psalm

God, my shepherd!
    I don't need a thing.
You have bedded me down in lush meadows,
    you find me quiet pools to drink from.
True to your word,
    you let me catch my breath
    and send me in the right direction.

Even when the way goes through
    Death Valley,
I'm not afraid
    when you walk at my side.
Your trusty shepherd's crook
    makes me feel secure.

You serve me a six-course dinner
    right in front of my enemies.
You revive my drooping head;
    my cup brims with blessing.

Your beauty and love chase after me
    every day of my life.
I'm back home in the house of GOD
    for the rest of my life.

24

A David psalm

GOD claims Earth and everything in it,
    GOD claims World and all who live on it.
He built it on Ocean foundations,
    laid it out on River girders.

Who can climb Mount GOD?
    Who can scale the holy north-face?
Only the clean-handed,
    only the pure-hearted;
Men who won't cheat,
    women who won't seduce.

GOD is at their side;
    with GOD's help they make it.
This, Jacob, is what happens
    to God-seekers, God-questers.

Wake up, you sleepyhead city!
Wake up, you sleepyhead people!
    King-Glory is ready to enter.

Who is this King-Glory?
    GOD, armed
    and battle-ready.

Wake up, you sleepyhead city!
Wake up, you sleepyhead people!
    King-Glory is ready to enter.

Who is this King-Glory?
    GOD-of-the-Angel-Armies:
    he is King-Glory.

25

A David psalm

My head is high, GOD, held high;
I'm looking to you, GOD;
No hangdog skulking for me.

I've thrown in my lot with you;
You won't embarrass me, will you?
Or let my enemies get the best of me?

Don't embarrass any of us
Who went out on a limb for you.
It's the traitors who should be humiliated.

Show me how you work, GOD;
School me in your ways.

Take me by the hand;
Lead me down the path of truth.
You are my Savior, aren't you?

Mark the milestones of your mercy and love, GOD;
Rebuild the ancient landmarks!

Forget that I sowed wild oats;
Mark me with your sign of love.
Plan only the best for me, GOD!

GOD is fair and just;
He corrects the misdirected,
Sends them in the right direction.

He gives the rejects his hand,
And leads them step by step.

From now on every road you travel
Will take you to GOD.
Follow the Covenant signs;
Read the charted directions.

Keep up your reputation, GOD;
Forgive my bad life;
It's been a very bad life.

My question: What are God-worshipers like?
Your answer: Arrows aimed at God's bull's-eye.

They settle down in a promising place;
Their kids inherit a prosperous farm.

God-friendship is for God-worshipers;
They are the ones he confides in.

If I keep my eyes on GOD,
I won't trip over my own feet.

Look at me and help me!
I'm all alone and in big trouble.

My heart and mind are fighting each other;
Call a truce to this civil war.

Take a hard look at my life of hard labor,
Then lift this ton of sin.

Do you see how many people
Have it in for me?
How viciously they hate me?

Keep watch over me and keep me out of trouble;
Don't let me down when I run to you.

Use all your skill to put me together;
I wait to see your finished product.

GOD, give your people a break
From this run of bad luck.

26

A David psalm

Clear my name, GOD;
    I've kept an honest shop.
I've thrown in my lot with you, GOD, and
    I'm not budging.

Examine me, GOD, from head to foot,
order your battery of tests.
Make sure I'm fit
inside and out

So I never lose
sight of your love,
But keep in step with you,
never missing a beat.

I don't hang out with tricksters,
I don't pal around with thugs;
I hate that pack of gangsters,
I don't deal with double-dealers.

I scrub my hands with purest soap,
then join hands with the others in the great
circle,
dancing around your altar, GOD,
Singing God-songs at the top of my lungs,
telling God-stories.

GOD, I love living with you;
your house glows with your glory.
When it's time for spring cleaning,
don't sweep me out with the quacks and crooks,
Men with bags of dirty tricks,
women with purses stuffed with bribe-money.

You know I've been aboveboard with you;
now be aboveboard with me.

I'm on the level with you, GOD;
I bless you every chance I get.

27

A David psalm

Light, space, zest—
that's GOD!
So, with him on my side I'm fearless,
afraid of no one and nothing.

When vandal hordes ride down
ready to eat me alive,
Those bullies and toughs
fall flat on their faces.

When besieged,
I'm calm as a baby.
When all hell breaks loose,
I'm collected and cool.

I'm asking GOD for one thing,
only one thing:
To live with him in his house
my whole life long.
I'll contemplate his beauty;
I'll study at his feet.

That's the only quiet, secure place
in a noisy world,

The perfect getaway,
far from the buzz of traffic.

God holds me head and shoulders
above all who try to pull me down.
I'm headed for his place to offer anthems
that will raise the roof!
Already I'm singing God-songs;
I'm making music to GOD.

Listen, GOD, I'm calling at the top of my lungs:
"Be good to me! Answer me!"
When my heart whispered, "Seek God,"
my whole being replied,
"I'm seeking him!"
Don't hide from me now!

You've always been right there for me;
don't turn your back on me now.
Don't throw me out, don't abandon me;
you've always kept the door open.
My father and mother walked out and left me,
but GOD took me in.

Point me down your highway, GOD;
direct me along a well-lighted street;
show my enemies whose side you're on.
Don't throw me to the dogs,
those liars who are out to get me,
filling the air with their threats.

I'm sure now I'll see God's goodness
in the exuberant earth.
Stay with GOD!
Take heart. Don't quit.
I'll say it again:
Stay with GOD.

28

A David psalm

Don't turn a deaf ear
when I call you, GOD.
If all I get from you is
deafening silence,
I'd be better off
in the Black Hole.

I'm letting you know what I need,
calling out for help
And lifting my arms
toward your inner sanctuary.

Don't shove me into
the same jail cell with those crooks,
With those who are
full-time employees of evil.
They talk a good line of "peace,"
then moonlight for the Devil.

Pay them back for what they've done,
for how bad they've been.

Pay them back for their long hours
in the Devil's workshop;
Then cap it with a huge bonus.

Because they have no idea how God works
or what he is up to,
God will smash them to smithereens
and walk away from the ruins.

Blessed be GOD—
he heard me praying.
He proved he's on my side;
I've thrown my lot in with him.

Now I'm jumping for joy,
and shouting and singing my thanks to him.

GOD is all strength for his people,
ample refuge for his chosen leader;
Save your people
and bless your heritage.
Care for them;
carry them like a good shepherd.

29

A David psalm

Bravo, GOD, bravo!
Gods and all angels shout, "Encore!"

In awe before the glory,
    in awe before God's visible power.
Stand at attention!
    Dress your best to honor him!

GOD thunders across the waters,
Brilliant, his voice and his face, streaming brightness—
GOD, across the flood waters.

GOD's thunder tympanic,
GOD's thunder symphonic.

GOD's thunder smashes cedars,
GOD topples the northern cedars.

The mountain ranges skip like spring colts,
The high ridges jump like wild kid goats.

GOD's thunder spits fire.
GOD thunders, the wilderness quakes;
He makes the desert of Kadesh shake.

GOD's thunder sets the oak trees dancing
A wild dance, whirling; the pelting rain strips their
        branches.
We fall to our knees—we call out, "Glory!"

Above the floodwaters is GOD's throne
    from which his power flows,
    from which he rules the world.

God makes his people strong.
God gives his people peace.

30

A David psalm

I give you all the credit, God—
    you got me out of that mess,
    you didn't let my foes gloat.

God, my God, I yelled for help
    and you put me together.
God, you pulled me out of the grave,
    gave me another chance at life
    when I was down and out.

All you saints! Sing your hearts out to God!
    Thank him to his face!
He gets angry once in a while, but across
    a lifetime there is only love.
The nights of crying your eyes out
    give way to days of laughter.

When things were going great
    I crowed, "I've got it made.
I'm God's favorite.
    He made me king of the mountain."
Then you looked the other way
    and I fell to pieces.

I called out to you, GOD;
    I laid my case before you:
"Can you sell me for a profit when I'm dead?
    auction me off at a cemetery yard sale?
When I'm 'dust to dust' my songs
    and stories of you won't sell.
So listen! and be kind!
    Help me out of this!"

You did it: you changed wild lament
    into whirling dance;
You ripped off my black mourning band
    and decked me with wildflowers.
I'm about to burst with song;
    I can't keep quiet about you.
GOD, my God,
    I can't thank you enough.

31

A David psalm

I run to you, GOD; I run for dear life.
    Don't let me down!
    Take me seriously this time!
Get down on my level and listen,
    and please—no procrastination!
Your granite cave a hiding place,
    your high cliff nest a place of safety.

You're my cave to hide in,
    my cliff to climb.

Be my safe leader,
    be my true mountain guide.
Free me from hidden traps;
    I want to hide in you.
I've put my life in your hands.
    You won't drop me,
    you'll never let me down.

I hate all this silly religion,
    but you, GOD, I trust.
I'm leaping and singing in the circle of your love;
    you saw my pain,
    you disarmed my tormentors,
You didn't leave me in their clutches
    but gave me room to breathe.
Be kind to me, GOD—
    I'm in deep, deep trouble again.
I've cried my eyes out;
    I feel hollow inside.
My life leaks away, groan by groan;
    my years fade out in sighs.
My troubles have worn me out,
    turned my bones to powder.
To my enemies I'm a monster;
    I'm ridiculed by the neighbors.
My friends are horrified;
    they cross the street to avoid me.
They want to blot me from memory,
    forget me like a corpse in a grave,
    discard me like a broken dish in the trash.

The street-talk gossip has me
    "criminally insane"!
Behind locked doors they plot
    how to ruin me for good.

Desperate, I throw myself on you:
    you are my God!
Hour by hour I place my days in your hand,
    safe from the hands out to get me.
Warm me, your servant, with a smile;
    save me because you love me.
Don't embarrass me by not showing up;
    I've given you plenty of notice.
Embarrass the wicked, stand them up,
    leave them stupidly shaking their heads
    as they drift down to hell.
Gag those loudmouthed liars
    who heckle me, your follower,
    with jeers and catcalls.

What a stack of blessing you have piled up
    for those who worship you,
Ready and waiting for all who run to you
    to escape an unkind world.
You hide them safely away
    from the opposition.
As you slam the door on those oily, mocking faces,
    you silence the poisonous gossip.
Blessed GOD!
    His love is the wonder of the world.

Trapped by a siege, I panicked.
    "Out of sight, out of mind," I said.
But you heard me say it,
    you heard and listened.

Love God, all you saints;
    God takes care of all who stay close to him,
But he pays back in full
    those arrogant enough to go it alone.

Be brave. Be strong. Don't give up.
    Expect God to get here soon.

32

A David psalm

Count yourself lucky, how happy you must be—
    you get a fresh start,
    your slate's wiped clean.

Count yourself lucky—
    God holds nothing against you
    and you're holding nothing back from him.

When I kept it all inside,
    my bones turned to powder,
    my words became daylong groans.

The pressure never let up;
    all the juices of my life dried up.

Then I let it all out;
I said, "I'll come clean about my failures to
GOD."

Suddenly the pressure was gone—
my guilt dissolved,
my sin disappeared.

These things add up. Every one of us needs to pray;
when all hell breaks loose and the dam bursts
we'll be on high ground, untouched.

GOD's my island hideaway,
keeps danger far from the shore,
throws garlands of hosannas around my neck.

Let me give you some good advice;
I'm looking you in the eye
and giving it to you straight:

"Don't be ornery like a horse or mule
that needs bit and bridle
to stay on track."

God-defiers are always in trouble;
GOD-affirmers find themselves loved
every time they turn around.

Celebrate GOD.
Sing together—everyone!
All you honest hearts, raise the roof!

33

Good people, cheer GOD!
Right-living people sound best when praising.
Use guitars to reinforce your Hallelujahs!
Play his praise on a grand piano!
Compose your own new song to him;
give him a trumpet fanfare.

For GOD's Word is solid to the core;
everything he makes is sound inside and out.
He loves it when everything fits,
when his world is in plumb-line true.
Earth is drenched
in GOD's affectionate satisfaction.

The skies were made by GOD's command;
he breathed the word and the stars popped out.
He scooped Sea into his jug,
put Ocean in his keg.

Earth-creatures, bow before GOD;
world-dwellers—down on your knees!
Here's why: he spoke and there it was,
in place the moment he said so.

GOD takes the wind out of Babel pretense,
he shoots down the world's power-schemes.
GOD's plan for the world stands up,
all his designs are made to last.

Blessed is the country with GOD for God;
blessed are the people he's put in his will.

From high in the skies GOD looks around,
he sees all Adam's brood.
From where he sits
he overlooks all us earth-dwellers.
He has shaped each person in turn;
now he watches everything we do.

No king succeeds with a big army alone,
no warrior wins by brute strength.
Horsepower is not the answer;
no one gets by on muscle alone.

Watch this: God's eye is on those who respect him,
the ones who are looking for his love.
He's ready to come to their rescue in bad times;
in lean times he keeps body and soul together.

We're depending on GOD;
he's everything we need.
What's more, our hearts brim with joy
since we've taken for our own his holy name.
Love us, GOD, with all you've got—
that's what we're depending on.

34

A David psalm, when he outwitted Abimelech and got away

I bless GOD every chance I get;
my lungs expand with his praise.

I live and breathe GOD;
if things aren't going well, hear this and be happy:

Join me in spreading the news;
together let's get the word out.

GOD met me more than halfway,
he freed me from my anxious fears.

Look at him; give him your warmest smile.
Never hide your feelings from him.

When I was desperate, I called out,
and GOD got me out of a tight spot.

GOD's angel sets up a circle
of protection around us while we pray.

Open your mouth and taste, open your eyes and see—
how good GOD is.
Blessed are you who run to him.

Worship GOD if you want the best;
worship opens doors to all his goodness.

Young lions on the prowl get hungry,
but GOD-seekers are full of God.

Come, children, listen closely;
I'll give you a lesson in GOD worship.

Who out there has a lust for life?
Can't wait each day to come upon beauty?

Guard your tongue from profanity,
and no more lying through your teeth.

Turn your back on sin; do something good.
Embrace peace—don't let it get away!

God keeps an eye on his friends,
his ears pick up every moan and groan.

God won't put up with rebels;
he'll cull them from the pack.

Is anyone crying for help? God is listening,
ready to rescue you.

If your heart is broken, you'll find God right
there;
if you're kicked in the gut, he'll help you catch
your breath.

Disciples so often get into trouble;
still, God is there every time.

He's your bodyguard, shielding every bone;
not even a finger gets broken.

The wicked commit slow suicide;
they waste their lives hating the good.

God pays for each slave's freedom;
no one who runs to him loses out.

35

A David psalm

Harass these hecklers, GOD,
punch these bullies in the nose.
Grab a weapon, anything at hand;
stand up for me!
Get ready to throw the spear, aim the javelin,
at the people who are out to get me.
Reassure me; let me hear you say,
"I'll save you."

When those thugs try to knife me in the back,
make them look foolish.
Frustrate all those
who are plotting my downfall.
Make them like cinders in a high wind,
with GOD's angel working the bellows.
Make their road lightless and mud-slick,
with GOD's angel on their tails.
Out of sheer cussedness they set a trap to catch me;
for no good reason they dug a ditch to stop me.
Surprise them with your ambush—
catch them in the very trap they set,
the disaster they planned for me.

But let me run loose and free,
celebrating GOD's great work,
Every bone in my body laughing, singing, "GOD,
there's no one like you.

You put the down-and-out on their feet
    and protect the unprotected from bullies!"

Hostile accusers appear out of nowhere,
    they stand up and badger me.
They pay me back misery for mercy,
    leaving my soul empty.

When they were sick, I dressed in black;
    instead of eating, I prayed.
My prayers were like lead in my gut,
    like I'd lost my best friend, my brother.
I paced, distraught as a motherless child,
    hunched and heavyhearted.

But when I was down
    they threw a party!
All the nameless misfits of the town came
    chanting insults about me.
Like barbarians desecrating a shrine,
    they destroyed my reputation.

God, how long are you going
    to stand there doing nothing?
Save me from their brutalities;
    everything I've got is being thrown to the lions.
I will give you full credit
    when everyone gathers for worship;
When the people turn out in force
    I will say my Hallelujahs.

Don't let these liars, my enemies,
    have a party at my expense,
Those who hate me for no reason,
    winking and rolling their eyes.
No good is going to come
    from that crowd;
They spend all their time cooking up gossip
    against those who mind their own business.
They open their mouths
    in ugly grins,
Mocking, "Ha-ha, ha-ha, thought you'd get away
        with it?
    We've caught you hands down!"

Don't you see what they're doing, GOD?
    You're not going to let them
Get by with it, are you? Not going to walk off
    without *doing* something, are you?

Please get up—wake up! Tend to my case.
    My God, my Lord—my life is on the line.
Do what you think is right, GOD, my God,
    but don't make me pay for their good time.
Don't let them say to themselves,
    "Ha-ha, we got what we wanted."
Don't let them say,
    "We've chewed him up and spit him out."
Let those who are being hilarious
    at my expense
Be made to look ridiculous.

Make them wear donkey's ears;
Pin them with the donkey's tail,
who made themselves so high and mighty!

But those who want
the best for me,
Let them have the last word—a glad shout!—
and say, over and over and over,
"God is great—everything works
together for good for his servant."
I'll tell the world how great and good you are,
I'll shout Hallelujah all day, every day.

36

A David psalm

The God-rebel tunes in to sedition—
all ears, eager to sin.
He has no regard for God,
he stands insolent before him.
He has smooth-talked himself
into believing
That his evil
will never be noticed.
Words gutter from his mouth,
dishwater dirty.
Can't remember when he
did anything decent.
Every time he goes to bed,
he fathers another evil plot.

When he's loose on the streets,
    nobody's safe.
He plays with fire
    and doesn't care who gets burned.

God's love is meteoric,
    his loyalty astronomic,
His purpose titanic,
    his verdicts oceanic.
Yet in his largeness
    nothing gets lost;
Not a man, not a mouse,
    slips through the cracks.

How exquisite your love, O God!
    How eager we are to run under your wings,
To eat our fill at the banquet you spread
    as you fill our tankards with Eden spring
        water.
You're a fountain of cascading light,
    and you open our eyes to light.

Keep on loving your friends;
    do your work in welcoming hearts.
Don't let the bullies kick me around,
    the moral midgets slap me down.
Send the upstarts sprawling
    flat on their faces in the mud.

37

A David psalm

Don't bother your head with braggarts
or wish you could succeed like the wicked.
In no time they'll shrivel like grass clippings
and wilt like cut flowers in the sun.

Get insurance with GOD and do a good deed,
settle down and stick to your last.
Keep company with GOD,
get in on the best.

Open up before GOD, keep nothing back;
he'll do whatever needs to be done:
He'll validate your life in the clear light of day
and stamp you with approval at high noon.

Quiet down before GOD,
be prayerful before him.
Don't bother with those who climb the ladder,
who elbow their way to the top.

Bridle your anger, trash your wrath,
cool your pipes—it only makes things worse.
Before long the crooks will be bankrupt;
GOD-investors will soon own the store.

Before you know it, the wicked will have had it;
you'll stare at his once famous place and—
nothing!

Down-to-earth people will move in and take over,
relishing a huge bonanza.

Bad guys have it in for the good guys,
obsessed with doing them in.
But GOD isn't losing any sleep; to him
they're a joke with no punch line.

Bullies brandish their swords,
pull back on their bows with a flourish.
They're out to beat up on the harmless,
or mug that nice man out walking his dog.
A banana peel lands them flat on their faces—
slapstick figures in a moral circus.

Less is more and more is less.
One righteous will outclass fifty wicked,
For the wicked are moral weaklings
but the righteous are GOD-strong.

GOD keeps track of the decent folk;
what they do won't soon be forgotten.
In hard times, they'll hold their heads high;
when the shelves are bare, they'll be full.

God-despisers have had it;
GOD's enemies are finished—
Stripped bare like vineyards at harvesttime,
vanished like smoke in thin air.

Wicked borrows and never returns;
    Righteous gives and gives.
Generous gets it all in the end;
    Stingy is cut off at the pass.

Stalwart walks in step with God;
    his path blazed by God, he's happy.
If he stumbles, he's not down for long;
    God has a grip on his hand.

I once was young, now I'm a graybeard—
    not once have I seen an abandoned believer,
    or his kids out roaming the streets.
Every day he's out giving and lending,
    his children making him proud.

Turn your back on evil,
    work for the good and don't quit.
God loves this kind of thing,
    never turns away from his friends.

Live this way and you've got it made,
    but bad eggs will be tossed out.
The good get planted on good land
    and put down healthy roots.

Righteous chews on wisdom like a dog on a bone,
    rolls virtue around on his tongue.

His heart pumps God's Word like blood through
his veins;
his feet are as sure as a cat's.

Wicked sets a watch for Righteous,
he's out for the kill.
GOD, alert, is also on watch—
Wicked won't hurt a hair of his head.

Wait passionately for GOD,
don't leave the path.
He'll give you your place in the sun
while you watch the wicked lose it.

I saw Wicked bloated like a toad,
croaking pretentious nonsense.
The next time I looked there was nothing—
a punctured bladder, vapid and limp.

Keep your eye on the healthy soul,
scrutinize the straight life;
There's a future
in strenuous wholeness.
But the willful will soon be discarded;
insolent souls are on a dead-end street.

The spacious, free life is from GOD,
it's also protected and safe.
GOD-strengthened, we're delivered from evil—
when we run to him, he saves us.

38

A David psalm

Take a deep breath, God; calm down—
don't be so hasty with your punishing rod.
Your sharp-pointed arrows of rebuke draw blood;
my backside stings from your discipline.

I've lost twenty pounds in two months
because of your accusation.
My bones are brittle as dry sticks
because of my sin.
I'm swamped by my bad behavior,
collapsed under an avalanche of guilt.

The cuts in my flesh stink and grow maggots
because I've lived so badly.
And now I'm flat on my face
feeling sorry for myself morning to night.
All my insides are on fire,
my body is a wreck.
I'm on my last legs; I've had it—
my life is a vomit of groans.

Lord, my longings are sitting in plain sight,
my groans an old story to you.
My heart's about to break;
I'm a burned-out case.

Cataracts blind me to God and good;
    old friends avoid me like the plague.
My cousins never visit,
    my neighbors stab me in the back.
My competitors blacken my name,
    devoutly they pray for my ruin.
But I'm deaf and mute to it all,
    ears shut, mouth shut.
I don't hear a word they say,
    don't speak a word in response.
What I do, GOD, is wait for you,
    wait for my Lord, my God—you *will* answer!
I wait and pray so they won't laugh me off,
    won't smugly strut off when I stumble.

I'm on the edge of losing it—
    the pain in my gut keeps burning.
I'm ready to tell my story of failure,
    I'm no longer smug in my sin.
My enemies are alive and in action,
    a lynch mob after my neck.
I give out good and get back evil
    from God-haters who can't stand a God-lover.

Don't dump me, GOD;
    my God, don't stand me up.
Hurry and help me;
    I want some wide-open space in my life!

39

A David psalm

I'm determined to watch steps and tongue
so they won't land me in trouble.
I decided to hold my tongue
as long as Wicked is in the room.
"Mum's the word," I said, and kept quiet.
But the longer I kept silence
The worse it got—
my insides got hotter and hotter.
My thoughts boiled over;
I spilled my guts.

"Tell me, what's going on, GOD?
How long do I have to live?
Give me the bad news!
You've kept me on pretty short rations;
my life is string too short to be saved.
Oh! we're all puffs of air.
Oh! we're all shadows in a campfire.
Oh! we're just spit in the wind.
We make our pile, and then we leave it.

"What am I doing in the meantime, Lord?
Hoping, that's what I'm doing—hoping
You'll save me from a rebel life,
save me from the contempt of idiots.

I'll say no more, I'll shut my mouth,
    since you, Lord, are behind all this.
    But I can't take it much longer.
When you put us through the fire
    to purge us from our sin,
    our dearest idols go up in smoke.
Are we also nothing but smoke?

"Ah, God, listen to my prayer, my
    cry—open your ears.
Don't be callous;
    just look at these tears of mine.
I'm a stranger here. I don't know my way—
    a migrant like my whole family.
Give me a break, cut me some slack
    before it's too late and I'm out of here."

40

A David psalm

I waited and waited and waited for God.
    At last he looked; finally he listened.
He lifted me out of the ditch,
    pulled me from deep mud.
He stood me up on a solid rock
    to make sure I wouldn't slip.
He taught me how to sing the latest God-song,
    a praise-song to our God.
More and more people are seeing this:

they enter the mystery,
abandoning themselves to GOD.

Blessed are you who give yourselves over to GOD,
turn your backs on the world's "sure thing,"
ignore what the world worships;
The world's a huge stockpile
of GOD-wonders and God-thoughts.
Nothing and no one
compares to you!
I start talking about you, telling what I know,
and quickly run out of words.
Neither numbers nor words
account for you.

Doing something for you, bringing something to
you—
that's not what you're after.
Being religious, acting pious—
that's not what you're asking for.
You've opened my ears
so I can listen.

So I answered, "I'm coming.
I read in your letter what you wrote about me,
And I'm coming to the party
you're throwing for me."
That's when God's Word entered my life,
became part of my very being.

I've preached you to the whole congregation,
I've kept back nothing, GOD—you know that.
I didn't keep the news of your ways
a secret, didn't keep it to myself.
I told it all, how dependable you are, how
thorough.
I didn't hold back pieces of love and truth
For myself alone. I told it all,
let the congregation know the whole story.

Now GOD, don't hold out on me,
don't hold back your passion.
Your love and truth
are all that keeps me together.
When troubles ganged up on me,
a mob of sins past counting,
I was so swamped by guilt
I couldn't see my way clear.
More guilt in my heart than hair on my head,
so heavy the guilt that my heart gave out.

Soften up, GOD, and intervene;
hurry and get me some help,
So those who are trying to kidnap my soul
will be embarrassed and lose face,
So anyone who gets a kick out of making me
miserable
will be heckled and disgraced,
So those who pray for my ruin
will be booed and jeered without mercy.

But all who are hunting for you—
    oh, let them sing and be happy.
Let those who know what you're all about
    tell the world you're great and not quitting.
And me? I'm a mess. I'm nothing and have nothing:
    make something of me.
You can do it; you've got what it takes—
    but God, don't put it off.

41

A David psalm

Dignify those who are down on their luck;
    you'll feel good—*that's* what GOD does.
GOD looks after us all,
    makes us robust with life—
Lucky to be in the land,
    we're free from enemy worries.
Whenever we're sick and in bed,
    GOD becomes our nurse,
    nurses us back to health.

I said, "GOD, be gracious!
    Put me together again—
    my sins have torn me to pieces."
My enemies are wishing the worst for me;
    they make bets on what day I will die.
If someone comes to see me,
    he mouths empty platitudes,

All the while gathering gossip about me
    to entertain the street-corner crowd.
These "friends" who hate me
    whisper slanders all over town.
They form committees
    to plan misery for me.

The rumor goes out, "He's got some dirty,
    deadly disease. The doctors
    have given up on him."
Even my best friend, the one I always told
        everything
    —he ate meals at my house all the time!—
    has bitten my hand.

God, give grace, get me up on my feet.
    I'll show them a thing or two.

Meanwhile, I'm sure you're on my side—
    no victory shouts yet from the enemy camp!
You know me inside and out, you hold me
        together,
    you never fail to stand me tall in your presence
    so I can look you in the eye.

Blessed is God, Israel's God,
    always, always, always.
    Yes. Yes. Yes.

42

A psalm of the sons of Korah

A white-tailed deer drinks
    from the creek;
I want to drink God,
    deep drafts of God.
I'm thirsty for God-alive.
I wonder, "Will I ever make it—
    arrive and drink in God's presence?"
I'm on a diet of tears—
    tears for breakfast, tears for supper.
All day long
    people knock at my door,
Pestering,
    "Where is this God of yours?"

These are the things I go over and over,
    emptying out the pockets of my life.
I was always at the head of the worshiping crowd,
    right out in front,
Leading them all,
    eager to arrive and worship,
Shouting praises, singing thanksgiving—
    celebrating, all of us, God's feast!

Why are you down in the dumps, dear soul?
    Why are you crying the blues?

Fix my eyes on God—
soon I'll be praising again.
He puts a smile on my face.
He's my God.

When my soul is in the dumps, I rehearse
everything I know of you,
From Jordan depths to Hermon heights,
including Mount Mizar.
Chaos calls to chaos,
to the tune of whitewater rapids.
Your breaking surf, your thundering breakers
crash and crush me.
Then GOD promises to love me all day,
sing songs all through the night!
My life is God's prayer.

Sometimes I ask God, my rock-solid God,
"Why did you let me down?
Why am I walking around in tears,
harassed by enemies?"
They're out for the kill, these
tormentors with their obscenities,
Taunting day after day,
"Where is this God of yours?"

Why are you down in the dumps, dear soul?
Why are you crying the blues?
Fix my eyes on God—
soon I'll be praising again.

He puts a smile on my face.
He's my God.

43

Clear my name, God; stick up for me
against these loveless, immoral people.
Get me out of here, away
from these lying degenerates.
I counted on you, God.
Why did you walk out on me?
Why am I pacing the floor, wringing my hands
over these outrageous people?

Give me your lantern and compass,
give me a map,
So I can find my way to the sacred mountain,
to the place of your presence,
To enter the place of worship,
meet my exuberant God,
Sing my thanks with a harp,
magnificent God, my God.

Why are you down in the dumps, dear soul?
Why are you crying the blues?
Fix my eyes on God—
soon I'll be praising again.
He puts a smile on my face.
He's my God.

44

A psalm of the sons of Korah

We've been hearing about this, God,
all our lives.
Our fathers told us the stories
their fathers told them,
How single-handedly you weeded out the godless
from the fields and planted us,
How you sent those people packing
but gave us a fresh start.
We didn't fight for this land;
we didn't work for it—it was a gift!
You gave it, smiling as you gave it,
delighting as you gave it.

You're my King, O God—
command victories for Jacob!
With your help we'll wipe out our enemies,
in your name we'll stomp them to dust.
I don't trust in weapons;
my sword won't save me—
But it's you, you who saved us from the enemy;
you made those who hate us lose face.
All day we parade God's praise—
we thank you by name over and over.

But now you've walked off and left us,
you've disgraced us and won't fight for us.

You made us turn tail and run;
those who hate us have cleaned us out.
You delivered us as sheep to the butcher,
you scattered us to the four winds.
You sold your people at a discount—
you made nothing on the sale.

You made people on the street,
people we know, poke fun and call us names.
You made us a joke among the godless,
a cheap joke among the rabble.
Every day I'm up against it,
my nose rubbed in my shame—
Gossip and ridicule fill the air,
people out to get me crowd the street.

All this came down on us,
and we've done nothing to deserve it.
We never betrayed your Covenant: our hearts
were never false, our feet never left your path.
Do we deserve torture in a den of jackals?
or lockup in a black hole?

If we had forgotten to pray to our God
or made fools of ourselves with store-bought
gods,
Wouldn't God have figured this out?
We can't hide things from him.
No, you decided to make us martyrs,
lambs assigned for sacrifice each day.

Get up, God! Are you going to sleep all day?
    Wake up! Don't you care what happens to us?
Why do you bury your face in the pillow?
    Why pretend things are just fine with us?
And here we are—flat on our faces in the dirt,
    held down with a boot on our necks.
Get up and come to our rescue.
    If you love us so much, *Help us!*

45

A wedding song of the sons of Korah

My heart bursts its banks,
    spilling beauty and goodness.
I pour it out in a poem to the king,
    shaping the river into words:

"You're the handsomest of men;
    every word from your lips is sheer grace,
    and God has blessed you, blessed you so much.
Strap your sword to your side, warrior!
    Accept praise! Accept due honor!
    Ride majestically! Ride triumphantly!
Ride on the side of truth!
    Ride for the righteous meek!

"Your instructions are glow-in-the-dark;
    you shoot sharp arrows
Into enemy hearts; the king's
    foes lie down in the dust, beaten.

"Your throne is God's throne,
ever and always;
The scepter of your royal rule
measures right living.
You love the right
and hate the wrong.
And that is why God, your very own God,
poured fragrant oil on your head,
Marking you out as king
from among your dear companions.

"Your forest-drenched garments
are fragrant with mountain breeze.
Chamber music—from the throne room—
makes you want to dance.
Kings' daughters are maids in your court,
the Bride glittering with golden jewelry.

"Now listen, daughter, don't miss a word:
forget your country, put your home behind you.
Be *here*—the king is wild for you.
Since he's your lord, adore him.
Wedding gifts pour in from Tyre;
rich guests shower you with presents."

(Her wedding dress is dazzling,
lined with gold by the weavers;
All her dresses and robes
are woven with gold.

She is led to the king,
    followed by her virgin companions.
A procession of joy and laughter!
    a grand entrance to the king's palace!)

"Set your mind now on sons—
    don't dote on father and grandfather.
You'll set your sons up as princes
    all over the earth.
I'll make you famous for generations;
    you'll be the talk of the town
    for a long, long time."

46

A song of the sons of Korah

God is a safe place to hide,
    ready to help when we need him.
We stand fearless at the cliff-edge of doom,
    courageous in seastorm and earthquake,
Before the rush and roar of oceans,
    the tremors that shift mountains.

    Jacob-wrestling God fights for us,
    GOD-of-Angel-Armies protects us.

River fountains splash joy, cooling God's city,
    this sacred haunt of the Most High.
God lives here, the streets are safe,
    God at your service from crack of dawn.

Godless nations rant and rave, kings and kingdoms
threaten,
but Earth does anything he says.

Jacob-wrestling God fights for us,
GOD-of-Angel-Armies protects us.

Attention, all! See the marvels of GOD!
He plants flowers and trees all over the earth,
Bans war from pole to pole,
breaks all the weapons across his knee.
"Step out of the traffic! Take a long,
loving look at me, your High God,
above politics, above everything."

Jacob-wrestling God fights for us,
GOD-of-Angel-Armies protects us.

47

A psalm of the sons of Korah

Applause, everyone. Bravo, bravissimo!
Shout God-songs at the top of your lungs!
GOD Most High is stunning,
astride land and ocean.
He crushes hostile people,
puts nations at our feet.
He set us at the head of the line,
prize-winning Jacob, his favorite.

Loud cheers as God climbs the mountain,
    a ram's horn blast at the summit.
Sing songs to God, sing out!
    Sing to our King, sing praise!
He's Lord over earth,
    so sing your best songs to God.
God is Lord of godless nations—
    sovereign, he's King of the mountain.
Princes from all over are gathered,
    people of Abraham's God.
The powers of earth are God's—
    he soars over all.

48

A psalm of the sons of Korah

God majestic,
    praise abounds in our God-city!
His sacred mountain,
    breathtaking in its heights—earth's joy.
Zion Mountain looms in the North,
    city of the world-King.
God in his citadel peaks
    undefeatable.

The kings got together,
    they united and came.
They took one look and shook their heads,
    they scattered and ran away.

They doubled up in pain
    like a woman having a baby.

You smashed the ships of Tarshish
    with a storm out of the East.
We heard about it, then we saw it
    with our eyes—
In GOD's city of Angel Armies,
    in the city our God
Set on firm foundations,
    firm forever.

We pondered your love-in-action, God,
    waiting in your temple:
Your name, God, evokes a train
    of Hallelujahs wherever
It is spoken, near and far;
    your arms are heaped with goodness-in-action.

Be glad, Zion Mountain;
    Dance, Judah's daughters!
    He does what he said he'd do!

Circle Zion, take her measure,
    count her fortress peaks,
Gaze long at her sloping bulwark,
    climb her citadel heights—
Then you can tell the next generation
    detail by detail the story of God,
Our God forever,
    who guides us till the end of time.

49

A psalm of the sons of Korah

Listen, everyone, listen—
    earth-dwellers, don't miss this.
All you haves
    and have-nots,
All together now: listen.

I set plainspoken wisdom before you,
    my heart-seasoned understandings of life.
I fine-tuned my ear to the sayings of the wise,
    I solve life's riddle with the help of a harp.

So why should I fear in bad times,
    hemmed in by enemy malice,
Shoved around by bullies,
    demeaned by the arrogant rich?

Really! There's no such thing as self-rescue,
    pulling yourself up by your bootstraps.
The cost of rescue is beyond our means,
    and even then it doesn't guarantee
Life forever, or insurance
    against the Black Hole.

Anyone can see that the brightest and best die,
    wiped out right along with fools and idiots.

They leave all their prowess behind,
move into their new home, The Coffin,
The cemetery their permanent address.
And to think they named counties after
themselves!

We aren't immortal. We don't last long.
Like our dogs, we age and weaken. And die.

This is what happens to those who live for the
moment,
who only look out for themselves:
Death herds them like sheep straight to hell;
they disappear down the gullet of the grave;
They waste away to nothing—
nothing left but a marker in a cemetery.
But me? God snatches me from the clutch of death,
he reaches down and grabs me.

So don't be impressed with those who get rich
and pile up fame and fortune.
They can't take it with them;
fame and fortune all get left behind.
Just when they think they've arrived
and folks praise them because they've made good,
They enter the family burial plot
where they'll never see sunshine again.

We aren't immortal. We don't last long.
Like our dogs, we age and weaken. And die.

50

An Asaph psalm

The God of gods—it's GOD!—speaks out,
shouts, "Earth!"
welcomes the sun in the east,
farewells the disappearing sun in the west.
From the dazzle of Zion,
God blazes into view.
Our God makes his entrance,
he's not shy in his coming.
Starbursts of fireworks precede him.

He summons heaven and earth as a jury,
he's taking his people to court:
"Round up my saints who swore
on the Bible their loyalty to me."

The whole cosmos attests to the fairness of this court,
that here *God* is judge.

"Are you listening, dear people? I'm getting ready
to speak;
Israel, I'm about ready to bring you to trial.
This is God, your God,
speaking to you.
I don't find fault with your acts of worship,
the frequent burnt sacrifices you offer.
But why should I want your blue-ribbon bull,
or more and more goats from your herds?

Every creature in the forest is mine,
  the wild animals on all the mountains.
I know every mountain bird by name;
  the scampering field mice are my friends.
If I get hungry, do you think I'd tell you?
  All creation and its bounty are mine.
Do you think I feast on venison?
  or drink drafts of goats' blood?
Spread for me a banquet of praise,
  serve High God a feast of kept promises,
And call for help when you're in trouble—
  I'll help you, and you'll honor me."

Next, God calls up the wicked:

"What are you up to, quoting my laws,
  talking like we are good friends?
You never answer the door when I call;
  you treat my words like garbage.
If you find a thief, you make him your buddy;
  adulterers are your friends of choice.
Your mouth drools filth;
  lying is a serious art form with you.
You stab your own brother in the back,
  rip off your little sister.
I kept a quiet patience while you did these things;
  you thought I went along with your game.
I'm calling you on the carpet, *now*,
  laying your wickedness out in plain sight.

"Time's up for playing fast and
loose with me.
I'm ready to pass sentence,
and there's no help in sight!
It's the praising life that honors me.
As soon as you set your foot on the Way,
I'll show you my salvation."

51

A David psalm, after he was confronted by Nathan about the affair with Bathsheba

Generous in love—God, give grace!
Huge in mercy—wipe out my bad record.
Scrub away my guilt,
soak out my sins in your laundry.
I know how bad I've been;
my sins are staring me down.

You're the One I've violated, and you've seen
it all, seen the full extent of my evil.
You have all the facts before you;
whatever you decide about me is fair.
I've been out of step with you for a long time,
in the wrong since before I was born.
What you're after is truth from the inside out.
Enter me, then; conceive a new, true life.

Soak me in your laundry and I'll come out clean,
scrub me and I'll have a snow-white life.

Tune me in to foot-tapping songs,
set these once-broken bones to dancing.
Don't look too close for blemishes,
give me a clean bill of health.
God, make a fresh start in me,
shape a Genesis week from the chaos of my life.
Don't throw me out with the trash,
or fail to breathe holiness in me.
Bring me back from gray exile,
put a fresh wind in my sails!
Give me a job teaching rebels your ways
so the lost can find their way home.
Commute my death sentence, God, my salvation God,
and I'll sing anthems to your life-giving ways.
Unbutton my lips, dear God;
I'll let loose with your praise.

Going through the motions doesn't please you,
a flawless performance is nothing to you.
I learned God-worship
when my pride was shattered.
Heart-shattered lives ready for love
don't for a moment escape God's notice.

Make Zion the place you delight in,
repair Jerusalem's broken-down walls.
Then you'll get real worship from us,
acts of worship small and large,
Including all the bulls
they can heave onto your altar!

52

A David psalm, when Doeg the Edomite reported to Saul, "David's at Ahimelech's house"

Why do you brag of evil, "Big Man"?
God's mercy carries the day.
You scheme catastrophe;
your tongue cuts razor-sharp,
artisan in lies.
You love evil more than good,
you call black white.
You love malicious gossip,
you foul-mouth.

God will tear you limb from limb,
sweep you up and throw you out,
Pull you up by the roots
from the land of life.

Good people will watch and
worship. They'll laugh in relief:
"Big Man bet on the wrong horse,
trusted in big money,
made his living from catastrophe."

And I'm an olive tree,
growing green in God's house.
I trusted in the generous mercy
of God then and now.

I thank you always
    that you went into action.
And I'll stay right here,
    your good name my hope,
    in company with your faithful friends.

53

A David psalm

Bilious and bloated, they gas,
    "God is gone."
It's poison gas—
    they foul themselves, they poison
Rivers and skies;
    thistles are their cash crop.

God sticks his head out of heaven.
    He looks around.
He's looking for someone not stupid—
    one man, even, God-expectant,
    just one God-ready woman.

He comes up empty. A string
    of zeros. Useless, unshepherded
Sheep, taking turns pretending
    to be Shepherd.
The ninety and nine
    follow the one.

Don't they know anything,
    all these predators?

Don't they know
    they can't get away with this,
Treating people like a fast-food meal
    over which they're too busy to pray?

Night is coming for them, and nightmare—
    a nightmare they'll never wake up from.
God will make hash of these squatters,
    send them packing for good.

Is there anyone around to save Israel?
    God turns life around.
Turned-around Jacob skips rope,
    turned-around Israel sings laughter.

54

A David psalm, when the Ziphites reported to Saul, "David is hiding out with us"

God, for your sake, help me!
    Use your influence to clear me.
Listen, God—I'm desperate.
    Don't be too busy to hear me.

Outlaws are out to get me,
    hit men are trying to kill me.
Nothing will stop them;
    God means nothing to them.

Oh, look! God's right here helping!
    GOD's on my side,

Evil is looping back on my enemies.
  Don't let up! Finish them off!

I'm ready now to worship, so ready.
  I thank you, GOD—you're so good.
You got me out of every scrape,
  and I saw my enemies get it.

55

A David psalm

Open your ears, God, to my prayer;
  don't pretend you don't hear me knocking.
Come close and whisper your answer.
  I really need you.
I shudder at the mean voice,
  quail before the evil eye,
As they pile on the guilt,
  stockpile angry slander.

My insides are turned inside out;
  specters of death have me down.
I shake with fear,
  I shudder from head to foot.
"Who will give me wings," I ask—
  "wings like a dove?"
Get me out of here on dove wings;
  I want some peace and quiet.
I want a walk in the country,
  I want a cabin in the woods.

I'm desperate for a change
  from rage and stormy weather.

Come down hard, Lord—slit their tongues.
  I'm appalled how they've split the city
Into rival gangs
  prowling the alleys
Day and night spoiling for a fight,
  trash piled in the streets,
Even shopkeepers gouging and cheating
  in broad daylight.

This isn't the neighborhood bully
  mocking me—I could take that.
This isn't a foreign devil spitting
  invective—I could tune that out.
It's *you*! We grew up together!
  You! My best friend!
Those long hours of leisure as we walked
  arm in arm, God a third party to our conversation.

Haul my betrayers off alive to hell—let them
  experience the horror, let them
  feel every desolate detail of a damned life.

I call to God;
  GOD will help me.
At dusk, dawn, and noon I sigh
  deep sighs—he hears, he rescues.
My life is well and whole, secure
  in the middle of danger

Even while thousands
    are lined up against me.
God hears it all, and from his judge's bench
    puts them in their place.
But, set in their ways, they won't change;
    they pay him no mind.

And this, my best friend, betrayed his best friends;
    his life betrayed his word.
All my life I've been charmed by his speech,
    never dreaming he'd turn on me.
His words, which were music to my ears,
    turned to daggers in my heart.

Pile your troubles on GOD's shoulders—
    he'll carry your load, he'll help you out.
He'll never let good people
    topple into ruin.
But you, God, will throw the others
    into a muddy bog,
Cut the lifespan of assassins
    and traitors in half.

And I trust in you.

56

A David psalm, when he was captured by the Philistines in Gath

Take my side, God—I'm getting kicked around,
    stomped on every day.

Not a day goes by
    but somebody beats me up;
They make it their duty
    to beat me up.
When I get really afraid
    I come to you in trust.
I'm proud to praise God;
    fearless now, I trust in God.
    What can mere mortals do?

They don't let up—
    they smear my reputation
    and huddle to plot my collapse.
They gang up,
    sneak together through the alleys
To take me by surprise,
    wait their chance to get me.

Pay them back in evil!
    Get angry, God!
    Down with these people!

You've kept track of my every toss and turn
    through the sleepless nights,
Each tear entered in your ledger,
    each ache written in your book.

If my enemies run away,
    turn tail when I yell at them,
Then I'll know
    that God is on my side.

I'm proud to praise God,
    proud to praise GOD.
Fearless now, I trust in God;
    what can mere mortals do to me?

God, you did everything you promised,
    and I'm thanking you with all my heart.
You pulled me from the brink of death,
    my feet from the cliff-edge of doom.
Now I stroll at leisure with God
    in the sunlit fields of life.

57

A David psalm, when he hid in a cave from Saul

Be good to me, God—and now!
    I've run to you for dear life.
I'm hiding out under your wings
    until the hurricane blows over.
I call out to High God,
    the God who holds me together.
He sends orders from heaven and saves me,
    he humiliates those who kick me around.
God delivers generous love,
    he makes good on his word.

I find myself in a pride of lions
    who are wild for a taste of human flesh;
Their teeth are lances and arrows,
    their tongues are sharp daggers.

Soar high in the skies, O God!
    Cover the whole earth with your glory!

They booby-trapped my path;
    I thought I was dead and done for.
They dug a mantrap to catch me,
    and fell in headlong themselves.

I'm ready, God, so ready,
    ready from head to toe,
Ready to sing, ready to raise a tune:
    "Wake up, soul!
Wake up, harp! wake up, lute!
    Wake up, you sleepyhead sun!"

I'm thanking you, God, out loud in the streets,
    singing your praises in town and country.
The deeper your love, the higher it goes;
    every cloud is a flag to your faithfulness.

Soar high in the skies, O God!
    Cover the whole earth with your glory!

58

A David psalm

Is this any way to run a country?
    Is there an honest politician in the house?

Behind the scenes you weave webs of deceit,
behind closed doors you make deals with
demons.

The wicked crawl from the wrong side of the cradle;
their first words out of the womb are lies.
Poison, lethal rattlesnake poison,
drips from their forked tongues—
Deaf to threats, deaf to charm,
decades of wax built up in their ears.

God, smash their teeth to bits,
leave them toothless tigers.
Let their lives be buckets of water spilled,
all that's left, a damp stain in the sand.
Let them be trampled grass
worn smooth by the traffic.
Let them dissolve into snail slime,
be a miscarried fetus that never sees sunlight.
Before what they cook up is half-done, God,
throw it out with the garbage!

The righteous will call up their friends
when they see the wicked get their reward,
Serve up their blood in goblets
as they toast one another,
Everyone cheering, "It's worth it to play by the
rules!
God's handing out trophies and tending the
earth!"

59

A David psalm, when Saul set a watch on David's house in order to kill him

My God! Rescue me from my enemies,
    defend me from these mutineers.
Rescue me from their dirty tricks,
    save me from their hit men.

Desperadoes have ganged up on me,
    they're hiding in ambush for me.
I did nothing to deserve this, GOD,
    crossed no one, wronged no one.
All the same, they're after me,
    determined to get me.

Wake up and see for yourself! You're GOD,
    GOD-of-Angel-Armies, Israel's God!
Get on the job and take care of these pagans,
    don't be soft on these hard cases.

    They return when the sun goes down,
    They howl like coyotes, ringing the city.
    Then suddenly they're all at the gate,
    Snarling invective, drawn daggers in their teeth.
    They think they'll never get caught.

But you, GOD, break out laughing;
    you treat the godless nations like jokes.

Strong God, I'm watching you do it,
  I can always count on you.
God in dependable love shows up on time,
  shows me my enemies in ruin.

Don't make quick work of them, GOD,
  lest my people forget.
Bring them down in slow motion,
  take them apart piece by piece.
Let all their mean-mouthed arrogance
  catch up with them,
Catch them out and bring them down
  —every muttered curse
  —every barefaced lie.
Finish them off in fine style!
  Finish them off for good!
Then all the world will see
  that God rules well in Jacob,
  everywhere that God's in charge.

  They return when the sun goes down,
  They howl like coyotes, ringing the city.
  They scavenge for bones,
  And bite the hand that feeds them.

And me? I'm singing your prowess,
  shouting at dawn your largesse,
For you've been a safe place for me,
  a good place to hide.
Strong God, I'm watching you do it,

I can always count on you—
God, my dependable love.

60

A David psalm, when he fought against Aram-naharaim and Aram-zobah and Joab killed twelve thousand Edomites at the Valley of Salt

God! you walked off and left us,
kicked our defenses to bits
And stomped off angry.
Come back. Oh please, come back!

You shook earth to the foundations,
ripped open huge crevasses.
Heal the breaks! Everything's
coming apart at the seams.

You made your people look doom in the face,
then gave us cheap wine to drown our troubles.
Then you planted a flag to rally your people,
an unfurled flag to look to for courage.
Now do something quickly, answer right now,
so the one you love best is saved.

That's when God spoke in holy splendor,
"Bursting with joy,
I make a present of Shechem,
I hand out Succoth Valley as a gift.
Gilead's in my pocket,
to say nothing of Manasseh.

Ephraim's my hard hat,
Judah my hammer;
Moab's a scrub bucket,
I mop the floor with Moab,
Spit on Edom,
rain fireworks all over Philistia."

Who will take me to the thick of the fight?
Who'll show me the road to Edom?
You aren't giving up on us, are you, God?
refusing to go out with our troops?

Give us help for the hard task;
human help is worthless.
In God we'll do our very best;
he'll flatten the opposition for good.

61

A David psalm

God, listen to me shout,
bend an ear to my prayer.
When I'm far from anywhere,
down to my last gasp,
I call out, "Guide me
up High Rock Mountain!"

You've always given me breathing room,
a place to get away from it all,

A lifetime pass to your safe-house,
  an open invitation as your guest.
You've always taken me seriously, God,
  made me welcome among those who know and
    love you.

Let the days of the king add up
  to years and years of good rule.
Set his throne in the full light of God;
  post Steady Love and Good Faith as lookouts,
And I'll be the poet who sings your glory—
  and live what I sing every day.

62

A David psalm

God, the one and only—
  I'll wait as long as he says.
Everything I need comes from him,
  so why not?
He's solid rock under my feet,
  breathing room for my soul,
An impregnable castle:
  I'm set for life.

How long will you gang up on me?
  How long will you run with the bullies?
There's nothing to you, any of you—
  rotten floorboards, worm-eaten rafters,

Anthills plotting to bring down mountains,
far gone in make-believe.
You talk a good line,
but every "blessing" breathes a curse.

God, the one and only—
I'll wait as long as he says.
Everything I hope for comes from him,
so why not?
He's solid rock under my feet,
breathing room for my soul,
An impregnable castle:
I'm set for life.

My help and glory are in God
—granite-strength and safe-harbor-God—
So trust him absolutely, people;
lay your lives on the line for him.
God is a safe place to be.

Man as such is smoke,
woman as such, a mirage.
Put them together, they're nothing;
two times nothing is nothing.

And a windfall, if it comes—
don't make too much of it.

God said this once and for all;
how many times

Have I heard it repeated?
    "Strength comes
Straight from God."

Love to you, Lord God!
    You pay a fair wage for a good day's work!

63

A David psalm, when he was out in the Judean wilderness

God—you're my God!
    I can't get enough of you!
I've worked up such hunger and thirst for God,
    traveling across dry and weary deserts.

So here I am in the place of worship, eyes open,
    drinking in your strength and glory.
In your generous love I am really living at last!
    My lips brim praises like fountains.
I bless you every time I take a breath;
    My arms wave like banners of praise to you.

I eat my fill of prime rib and gravy;
    I smack my lips. It's time to shout praises!
If I'm sleepless at midnight,
    I spend the hours in grateful reflection.
Because you've always stood up for me,
    I'm free to run and play.
I hold on to you for dear life,
    and you hold me steady as a post.

Those who are out to get me are marked for doom,
marked for death, bound for hell.
They'll die violent deaths;
jackals will tear them limb from limb.
But the king is glad in God;
his true friends spread the joy,
While small-minded gossips
are gagged for good.

64

A David psalm

Listen and help, O God.
I'm reduced to a whine
And a whimper, obsessed
with feelings of doomsday.

Don't let them find me—
the conspirators out to get me,
Using their tongues as weapons,
flinging poison words,
poison-tipped arrow-words.
They shoot from ambush,
shoot without warning,
not caring who they hit.
They keep fit doing calisthenics
of evil purpose,
They keep lists of the traps
they've secretly set.

They say to each other,
    "No one can catch us,
    no one can detect our perfect crime."
The Detective detects the mystery
    in the dark of the cellar heart.

The God of the Arrow shoots!
    They double up in pain,
Fall flat on their faces
    in full view of the grinning crowd.

Everyone sees it. God's
    work is the talk of the town.
Be glad, good people! Fly to GOD!
    Good-hearted people, make praise your habit.

65

A David psalm

Silence is praise to you,
    Zion-dwelling God,
And also obedience.
    You hear the prayer in it all.

We all arrive at your doorstep sooner
    or later, loaded with guilt,
Our sins too much for us—
    but you get rid of them once and for all.
Blessed are the chosen! Blessed the guest
    at home in your place!
We expect our fill of good things

in your house, your heavenly manse.
All your salvation wonders
are on display in your trophy room.
Earth-Tamer, Ocean-Pourer,
Mountain-Maker, Hill-Dresser,
Muzzler of sea storm and wave crash,
of mobs in noisy riot—
Far and wide they'll come to a stop,
they'll stare in awe, in wonder.
Dawn and dusk take turns
calling, "Come and worship."

Oh, visit the earth,
ask her to join the dance!
Deck her out in spring showers,
fill the God-River with living water.
Paint the wheat fields golden.
Creation was made for this!
Drench the plowed fields,
soak the dirt clods
With rainfall as harrow and rake
bring her to blossom and fruit.
Snow-crown the peaks with splendor,
scatter rose petals down your paths,
All through the wild meadows, rose petals.
Set the hills to dancing,
Dress the canyon walls with live sheep,
a drape of flax across the valleys.
Let them shout, and shout, and shout!
Oh, oh, let them sing!

66

All together now—applause for God!
    Sing songs to the tune of his glory,
    set glory to the rhythms of his praise.
Say of God, "We've never seen anything like him!"
    When your enemies see you in action,
    they slink off like scolded dogs.
The whole earth falls to its knees—
    it worships you, sings to you,
    can't stop enjoying your name and fame.

Take a good look at God's wonders—
    they'll take your breath away.
He converted sea to dry land;
    travelers crossed the river on foot.
    Now isn't that cause for a song?

Ever sovereign in his high tower, he keeps
    his eye on the godless nations.
Rebels don't dare
    raise a finger against him.

Bless our God, oh peoples!
    Give him a thunderous welcome!
Didn't he set us on the road to life?
    Didn't he keep us out of the ditch?
He trained us first,
    passed us like silver through refining fires,

Brought us into hardscrabble country,
pushed us to our very limit,
Road-tested us inside and out,
took us to hell and back;
Finally he brought us
to this well-watered place.

I'm bringing my prizes and presents to your house.
I'm doing what I said I'd do,
What I solemnly swore I'd do
that day when I was in so much trouble:
The choicest cuts of meat
for the sacrificial meal;
Even the fragrance
of roasted lamb is like a meal!
Or make it an ox
garnished with goat meat!

All believers, come here and listen,
let me tell you what God did for me.
I called out to him with my mouth,
my tongue shaped the sounds of music.
If I had been cozy with evil,
the Lord would never have listened.
But he most surely *did* listen,
he came on the double when he heard my
prayer.
Blessed be God: he didn't turn a deaf ear,
he stayed with me, loyal in his love.

67

God, mark us with grace
  and blessing! Smile!
The whole country will see how you work,
  all the godless nations see how you save.
God! Let people thank and enjoy you.
  Let all people thank and enjoy you.
Let all far-flung people become happy
  and shout their happiness because
You judge them fair and square,
  you tend the far-flung peoples.
God! Let people thank and enjoy you.
  Let all people thank and enjoy you.
Earth, display your exuberance!
  You mark us with blessing, O God, our God.
You mark us with blessing, O God.
  Earth's four corners—honor him!

68

A David psalm

Up with God!
  Down with his enemies!
    Adversaries, run for the hills!
Gone like a puff of smoke,
  like a blob of wax in the fire—
    one look at God and the wicked vanish.

When the righteous see God in action
they'll laugh, they'll sing,
they'll laugh and sing for joy.
Sing hymns to God;
all heaven, sing out;
clear the way for the coming of Cloud-Rider.
Enjoy God,
cheer when you see him!

Father of orphans,
champion of widows,
is God in his holy house.
God makes homes for the homeless,
leads prisoners to freedom,
but leaves rebels to rot in hell.

God, when you took the lead with your people,
when you marched out into the wild,
Earth shook, sky broke out in a sweat;
God was on the march.
Even Sinai trembled at the sight of God on the move,
at the sight of Israel's God.
You pour out rain in buckets, O God;
thorn and cactus become an oasis
For your people to camp in and enjoy.
You set them up in business;
they went from rags to riches.

The Lord gave the word;
thousands called out the good news:

"Kings of the armies
    are on the run, on the run!"
While housewives, safe and sound back home,
    divide up the plunder,
    the plunder of Canaanite silver and gold.

The day Shaddai scattered the kings,
    snow fell on Black Mountain—
A huge mountain, this dragon mountain,
    a mighty mountain, this dragon mountain.
All you mountains not chosen,
    sulk now, and feel sorry for yourselves,
For this is the mountain God has chosen to live on;
    he'll rule from this mountain forever.

The chariots of God, twice ten thousand,
    and thousands more besides,
The Lord in the lead, riding down Sinai—
    straight to the Holy Place!
You climbed to the High Place, captives in tow,
    your arms full of plunder from rebels,
And now you sit there in state,
    GOD, sovereign GOD!

Blessed be the Lord—
    day after day he carries us along.
He's our Savior, our God, oh yes!
    He's God-for-us, he's God-who-saves-us.
Lord GOD knows all
    death's ins and outs.

What's more, he made heads roll,
    split the skulls of the enemy
As he marched out of heaven,
    saying, "I tied up the Dragon in knots,
    put a muzzle on the Deep Blue Sea."
You can wade through your enemies' blood,
    and your dogs taste of your enemies from your
        boots.

See God on parade
    to the sanctuary, my God,
    my King on the march!
Singers out front, the band behind,
    maidens in the middle with castanets.
The whole choir blesses God.
    Like a fountain of praise, Israel blesses
        GOD.
Look—little Benjamin's out
    front and leading
Princes of Judah in their royal robes,
    princes of Zebulun, princes of Naphtali.
Parade your power, O God,
    the power, O God, that made us what we are.
Your temple, High God, is Jerusalem;
    kings bring gifts to you.
Rebuke that old crocodile, Egypt,
    with her herd of wild bulls and calves,
Rapacious in her lust for silver,
    crushing peoples, spoiling for a fight.
Let Egyptian traders bring blue cloth

and Cush come running to God, her hands
outstretched.

Sing, oh kings of the earth!
Sing praises to the Lord!
There he is: Sky-Rider,
striding the ancient skies.
Listen—he's calling in thunder,
rumbling, rolling thunder.
Call out "Bravo!" to God,
the High God of Israel.
His splendor and strength
rise huge as thunderheads.

A terrible beauty, O God,
streams from your sanctuary.
It's Israel's strong God! He gives
power and might to his people!
Oh you, his people—bless God!

69

A David psalm

God, God, save me!
I'm in over my head,

Quicksand under me, swamp water over me;
I'm going down for the third time.

I'm hoarse from calling for help,
Bleary-eyed from searching the sky for God.

I've got more enemies than hairs on my head;
Liars and cheats are out to knife me in the back.

What I never stole
Must I now give back?

God, you know every sin I've committed;
My life's a wide-open book before you.

Don't let those who look to you in hope
Be discouraged by what happens to me,
Dear Lord! God of the armies!

Don't let those out looking for you
Come to a dead end by following me—
Please, dear God of Israel!

Because of you I look like an idiot,
I walk around ashamed to show my face.

My brothers shun me like a bum off the street;
My family treats me like an unwanted guest.

I love you more than I can say.
Because I'm madly in love with you,
They blame me for everything they dislike about
you.

When I poured myself out in prayer and fasting,
All it got me was more contempt.

When I put on a sad face,
They treated me like a clown.

Now drunks and gluttons
Make up drinking songs about me.

And me? I pray.
GOD, it's time for a break!

God, answer in love!
Answer with your sure salvation!

Rescue me from the swamp,
Don't let me go under for good,

Pull me out of the clutch of the enemy;
This whirlpool is sucking me down.

Don't let the swamp be my grave, the Black Hole
Swallow me, its jaws clenched around me.

Now answer me, GOD, because you love me;
Let me see your great mercy full-face.

Don't look the other way; your servant can't take it.
I'm in trouble. Answer right now!

Come close, God; get me out of here.
Rescue me from this deathtrap.

You know how they kick me around—
Pin on me the donkey's ears, the dunce's cap.

I'm broken by their taunts,
Flat on my face, reduced to a nothing.

I looked in vain for one friendly face. Not one.
I couldn't find one shoulder to cry on.

They put poison in my soup,
Vinegar in my drink.

Let their supper be bait in a trap that snaps shut;
May their best friends be trappers who'll skin them
alive.

Make them become blind as bats,
Give them the shakes from morning to night.

Let them know what you think of them,
Blast them with your red-hot anger.

Burn down their houses,
Leave them desolate with nobody at home.

They gossiped about the one you disciplined,
Made up stories about anyone wounded by God.

Pile on the guilt,
Don't let them off the hook.

Strike their names from the list of the living;
No rock-carved honor for them among the
righteous.

I'm hurt and in pain;
Give me space for healing, and mountain air.

Let me shout God's name with a praising song,
Let me tell his greatness in a prayer of thanks.

For GOD, this is better than oxen on the altar,
Far better than blue-ribbon bulls.

The poor in spirit see and are glad—
Oh, you God-seekers, take heart!

For GOD listens to the poor,
He doesn't walk out on the wretched.

You heavens, praise him; praise him, earth;
Also ocean and all things that swim in it.

For God is out to help Zion,
Rebuilding the wrecked towns of Judah.

Guess who will live there—
The proud owners of the land?

No, the children of his servants will get it,
The lovers of his name will live in it.

70

A David prayer

God! Please hurry to my rescue!
    GOD, come quickly to my side!
Those who are out to get me—
    let them fall all over themselves.
Those who relish my downfall—
    send them down a blind alley.
Give them a taste of their own medicine,
    those gossips off clucking their tongues.

Let those on the hunt for you
    sing and celebrate.
Let all who love your saving way
    say over and over, "God is mighty!"

But I've lost it. I'm wasted.
    God—quickly, quickly!
Quick to my side, quick to my rescue!
    GOD, don't lose a minute.

71

I run for dear life to GOD,
    I'll never live to regret it.
Do what you do so well:
    get me out of this mess and up on my feet.

Put your ear to the ground and listen,
    give me space for salvation.
Be a guest room where I can retreat;
    you said your door was always open!
You're my salvation—my vast, granite fortress.

My God, free me from the grip of Wicked,
    from the clutch of Bad and Bully.
You keep me going when times are tough—
    my bedrock, GOD, since my childhood.
I've hung on you from the day of my birth,
    the day you took me from the cradle;
    I'll never run out of praise.
Many gasp in alarm when they see me,
    but you take me in stride.

Just as each day brims with your beauty,
    my mouth brims with praise.
But don't turn me out to pasture when I'm old
    or put me on the shelf when I can't pull my
        weight.
My enemies are talking behind my back,
    watching for their chance to knife me.
The gossip is: "God has abandoned him.
    Pounce on him now; no one will help him."

God, don't just watch from the sidelines.
    Come on! Run to my side!
My accusers—make them lose face.
    Those out to get me—make them look

Like idiots, while I stretch out, reaching for you,
    and daily add praise to praise.
I'll write the book on your righteousness,
    talk up your salvation all the day long,
    never run out of good things to write or say.
I come in the power of the Lord God,
    I post signs marking his right-of-way.

You got me when I was an unformed youth,
    God, and taught me everything I know.
Now I'm telling the world your wonders;
    I'll keep at it until I'm old and gray.
God, don't walk off and leave me
    until I get out the news
Of your strong right arm to this world,
    news of your power to the world yet to come,
Your famous and righteous
    ways, O God.
God, you've done it all!
    Who is quite like you?
You, who made me stare trouble in the face,
    Turn me around;
Now let me look life in the face.
    I've been to the bottom;
Bring me up, streaming with honors;
    turn to me, be tender to me,
And I'll take up the lute and thank you
    to the tune of your faithfulness, God.
I'll make music for you on a harp,
    Holy One of Israel.

When I open up in song to you,
 I let out lungsful of praise,
 my rescued life a song.
All day long I'm chanting
 about you and your righteous ways,
While those who tried to do me in
 slink off looking ashamed.

72

A Solomon psalm

Give the gift of wise rule to the king, O God,
 the gift of just rule to the crown prince.
May he judge your people rightly,
 be honorable to your meek and lowly.
Let the mountains give exuberant witness;
 shape the hills with the contours of right living.
Please stand up for the poor,
 help the children of the needy,
 come down hard on the cruel tyrants.
Outlast the sun, outlive the moon—
 age after age after age.
Be rainfall on cut grass,
 earth-refreshing rain showers.
Let righteousness burst into blossom
 and peace abound until the moon fades to
 nothing.
Rule from sea to sea,
 from the River to the Rim.

Foes will fall on their knees before God,
his enemies lick the dust.
Kings remote and legendary will pay homage,
kings rich and resplendent will turn over their
wealth.
All kings will fall down and worship,
and godless nations sign up to serve him,
Because he rescues the poor at the first sign of need,
the destitute who have run out of luck.
He opens a place in his heart for the down-and-out,
he restores the wretched of the earth.
He frees them from tyranny and torture—
when they bleed, he bleeds;
when they die, he dies.

And live! Oh, let him live!
Deck him out in Sheba gold.
Offer prayers unceasing to him,
bless him from morning to night.
Fields of golden grain in the land,
cresting the mountains in wild exuberance,
Cornucopias of praise, praises
springing from the city like grass from the earth.
May he never be forgotten,
his fame shine on like sunshine.
May all godless people enter his circle of blessing
and bless the One who blessed them.

Blessed GOD, Israel's God,
the one and only wonder-working God!

Blessed always his blazing glory!
    All earth brims with his glory.
Yes and Yes and Yes.

73

An Asaph psalm

No doubt about it! God is good—
    good to good people, good to the good-hearted.
But I nearly missed it,
    missed seeing his goodness.
I was looking the other way,
    looking up to the people
At the top,
    envying the wicked who have it made,
Who have nothing to worry about,
    not a care in the whole wide world.

Pretentious with arrogance,
    they wear the latest fashions in violence,
Pampered and overfed,
    decked out in silk bows of silliness.
They jeer, using words to kill;
    they bully their way with words.
They're full of hot air,
    loudmouths disturbing the peace.
People actually listen to them—can you believe it?
    Like thirsty puppies, they lap up their words.

What's going on here? Is God out to lunch?
    Nobody's tending the store.
The wicked get by with everything;
    they have it made, piling up riches.
I've been stupid to play by the rules;
    what has it gotten me?
A long run of bad luck, that's what—
    a slap in the face every time I walk out the door.

If I'd have given in and talked like this,
    I would have betrayed your dear children.
Still, when I tried to figure it out,
    all I got was a splitting headache . . .
Until I entered the sanctuary of God.
    Then I saw the whole picture:
The slippery road you've put them on,
    with a final crash in a ditch of delusions.
In the blink of an eye, disaster!
    A blind curve in the dark, and—nightmare!
We wake up and rub our eyes. . . . Nothing.
    There's nothing to them. And there never was.

When I was beleaguered and bitter,
    totally consumed by envy,
I was totally ignorant, a dumb ox
    in your very presence.
I'm still in your presence,
    but you've taken my hand.
You wisely and tenderly lead me,
    and then you bless me.

You're all I want in heaven!
You're all I want on earth!
When my skin sags and my bones get brittle,
God is rock-firm and faithful.
Look! Those who left you are falling apart!
Deserters, they'll never be heard from again.
But I'm in the very presence of God—
oh, how refreshing it is!
I've made Lord God my home.
God, I'm telling the world what you do!

74

An Asaph psalm

You walked off and left us, and never looked back.
God, how could you do that?
We're your very own sheep;
how can you stomp off in anger?

Refresh your memory of us—you bought us a long time ago.
Your most precious tribe—you paid a good price for us!
Your very own Mount Zion—you actually lived here once!
Come and visit the site of disaster,
see how they've wrecked the sanctuary.

While your people were at worship, your enemies barged in,

brawling and scrawling graffiti.
They set fire to the porch;
axes swinging, they chopped up the woodwork,
Beat down the doors with sledgehammers,
then split them into kindling.
They burned your holy place to the ground,
violated the place of worship.
They said to themselves, "We'll wipe them all out,"
and burned down all the places of worship.

There's not a sign or symbol of God in sight,
nor anyone to speak in his name,
no one who knows what's going on.
How long, God, will barbarians blaspheme,
enemies curse and get by with it?
Why don't you do something? How long are you going
to sit there with your hands folded in your lap?
God is my King from the very start;
he works salvation in the womb of the earth.
With one blow you split the sea in two,
you made mincemeat of the dragon Tannin.
You lopped off the heads of Leviathan,
then served them up in a stew for the animals.
With your finger you opened up springs and creeks,
and dried up the wild floodwaters.
You own the day, you own the night;
you put stars and sun in place.
You laid out the four corners of earth,
shaped the seasons of summer and winter.

Mark and remember, GOD, all the enemy
taunts, each idiot desecration.
Don't throw your lambs to the wolves;
after all we've been through, don't forget us.
Remember your promises;
the city is in darkness, the countryside violent.
Don't leave the victims to rot in the street;
make them a choir that sings your praises.

On your feet, O God—
stand up for yourself!
Do you hear what they're saying about you,
all the vile obscenities?
Don't tune out their malicious filth,
the brawling invective that never lets up.

75

An Asaph psalm

We thank you, God, we thank you—
your Name is our favorite word;
your mighty works are all we talk about.

You say, "I'm calling this meeting to order,
I'm ready to set things right.
When the earth goes topsy-turvy
And nobody knows which end is up,
I nail it all down,
I put everything in place again.

I say to the smart alecks, 'That's enough,'
to the bullies, 'Not so fast.'"

Don't raise your fist against High God.
Don't raise your voice against Rock of Ages.
He's the One from east to west;
from desert to mountains, he's the One.

God rules: he brings this one down to his knees,
pulls that one up on her feet.
GOD has a cup in his hand,
a bowl of wine, full to the brim.
He draws from it and pours;
it's drained to the dregs.
Earth's wicked ones drink it all,
drink it down to the last bitter drop!

And I'm telling the story of God Eternal,
singing the praises of Jacob's God.
The fists of the wicked
are bloody stumps,
The arms of the righteous
are lofty green branches.

76

An Asaph psalm

God is well-known in Judah;
in Israel, he's a household name.

He keeps a house in Salem,
his own suite of rooms in Zion.
That's where, using arrows for kindling,
he made a bonfire of weapons of war.

Oh, how bright you shine!
Outshining their huge piles of loot!
The warriors were plundered
and left there impotent.
And now there's nothing to them,
nothing to show for their swagger and threats.
Your sudden roar, God of Jacob,
knocked the wind out of horse and rider.

Fierce you are, and fearsome!
Who can stand up to your rising anger?
From heaven you thunder judgment;
earth falls to her knees and holds her breath.
God stands tall and makes things right,
he saves all the wretched on earth.
Instead of smoldering rage—God-praise!
All that sputtering rage—now a garland for God!

Do for GOD what you said you'd do—
he is, after all, your God.
Let everyone in town bring offerings
to the One Who Watches our every move.
Nobody gets by with anything,
no one plays fast and loose with him.

77

An Asaph psalm

I yell out to my God, I yell with all my might,
I yell at the top of my lungs. He listens.

I found myself in trouble and went looking for my Lord;
my life was an open wound that wouldn't heal.
When friends said, "Everything will turn out all right,"
I didn't believe a word they said.
I remember God—and shake my head.
I bow my head—then wring my hands.
I'm awake all night—not a wink of sleep;
I can't even say what's bothering me.
I go over the days one by one,
I ponder the years gone by.
I strum my lute all through the night,
wondering how to get my life together.

Will the Lord walk off and leave us for good?
Will he never smile again?
Is his love worn threadbare?
Has his salvation promise burned out?
Has God forgotten his manners?
Has he angrily stomped off and left us?

"Just my luck," I said. "The High God retires
just the moment I need him."

Once again I'll go over what God has done,
lay out on the table the ancient wonders;
I'll ponder all the things you've accomplished,
and give a long, loving look at your acts.

Oh God! Your way is holy!
No god is great like God!
You're the God who makes things happen;
you showed everyone what you can do—
You pulled your people out of the worst kind of
trouble,
rescued the children of Jacob and Joseph.

Ocean saw you in action, God,
saw you and trembled with fear;
Deep Ocean was scared to death.
Clouds belched buckets of rain,
Sky exploded with thunder,
your arrows flashing this way and that.
From Whirlwind came your thundering voice,
Lightning exposed the world,
Earth reeled and rocked.
You strode right through Ocean,
walked straight through roaring Ocean,
but nobody saw you come or go.

Hidden in the hands of Moses and Aaron,
You led your people like a flock of sheep.

78

An Asaph psalm

Listen, dear friends, to God's truth,
bend your ears to what I tell you.
I'm chewing on the morsel of a proverb;
I'll let you in on the sweet old truths,
Stories we heard from our fathers,
counsel we learned at our mother's knee.
We're not keeping this to ourselves,
we're passing it along to the next generation—
GOD's fame and fortune,
the marvelous things he has done.

He planted a witness in Jacob,
set his Word firmly in Israel,
Then commanded our parents
to teach it to their children
So the next generation would know,
and all the generations to come—
Know the truth and tell the stories
so their children can trust in God,
Never forget the works of God
but keep his commands to the letter.
Heaven forbid they should be like their parents,
bullheaded and bad,
A fickle and faithless bunch
who never stayed true to God.

The Ephraimites, armed to the teeth,
ran off when the battle began.
They were cowards to God's Covenant,
refused to walk by his Word.
They forgot what he had done—
marvels he'd done right before their eyes.
He performed miracles in plain sight of their parents
in Egypt, out on the fields of Zoan.
He split the Sea and they walked right through it;
he piled the waters to the right and the left.
He led them by day with a cloud,
led them all the night long with a fiery torch.
He split rocks in the wilderness,
gave them all they could drink from underground springs;
He made creeks flow out from sheer rock,
and water pour out like a river.

All they did was sin even more,
rebel in the desert against the High God.
They tried to get their own way with God,
clamored for favors, for special attention.
They whined like spoiled children,
"Why can't God give us a decent meal in this desert?
Sure, he struck the rock and the water flowed,
creeks cascaded from the rock.
But how about some fresh-baked bread?
How about a nice cut of meat?"

When God heard that, he was furious—
his anger flared against Jacob,
he lost his temper with Israel.
It was clear they didn't believe God,
had no intention of trusting in his help.
But God helped them anyway, commanded the clouds
and gave orders that opened the gates of heaven.
He rained down showers of manna to eat,
he gave them the Bread of Heaven.
They ate the bread of the mighty angels;
he sent them all the food they could eat.
He let East Wind break loose from the skies,
gave a strong push to South Wind.
This time it was birds that rained down—
succulent birds, an abundance of birds.
He aimed them right for the center of their camp;
all round their tents there were birds.
They ate and had their fill;
he handed them everything they craved on a
platter.
But their greed knew no bounds;
they stuffed their mouths with more and more.
Finally, God was fed up, his anger erupted—
he cut down their brightest and best,
he laid low Israel's finest young men.

And—can you believe it?—they kept right on
sinning;
all those wonders and they still wouldn't
believe!

So their lives wasted away to nothing—
    nothing to show for their lives but a ghost town.
When he cut them down, they came running for
        help;
    they turned and pled for mercy.
They gave witness that God was their rock,
    that High God was their redeemer,
But they didn't mean a word of it;
    they lied through their teeth the whole time.
They could not have cared less about him,
    wanted nothing to do with his Covenant.

And God? Compassionate!
    Forgave the sin! Didn't destroy!
Over and over he reined in his anger,
    restrained his considerable wrath.
He knew what they were made of;
    he knew there wasn't much to them,
How often in the desert they had spurned him,
    tried his patience in those wilderness years.
Time and again they pushed him to the limit,
    provoked Israel's Holy God.
How quickly they forgot what he'd done,
    forgot their day of rescue from the enemy,
When he did miracles in Egypt,
    wonders on the plain of Zoan.
He turned the River and its streams to blood—
    not a drop of water fit to drink.
He sent flies, which ate them alive,
    and frogs, which drove them crazy.

He turned their harvest over to caterpillars,
everything they had worked for to the locusts.
He flattened their grapevines with hail;
a killing frost ruined their orchards.
He pounded their cattle with hail,
let thunderbolts loose on their herds.
His anger flared,
a wild firestorm of havoc,
An advance guard of disease-carrying angels
to clear the ground, preparing the way before him.
He didn't spare those people,
he let the plague rage through their lives.
He killed all the Egyptian firstborns,
lusty infants, offspring of Ham's virility.
Then he led his people out like sheep,
took his flock safely through the wilderness.
He took good care of them; they had nothing to fear.
The Sea took care of their enemies for good.
He brought them into his holy land,
this mountain he claimed for his own.
He scattered everyone who got in their way;
he staked out an inheritance for them—
the tribes of Israel all had their own places.

But they kept on giving him a hard time,
rebelled against God, the High God,
refused to do anything he told them.
They were worse, if that's possible, than their
parents:
traitors—crooked as a corkscrew.

Their pagan orgies provoked God's anger,
 their obscene idolatries broke his heart.
When God heard their carryings-on, he was furious;
 he posted a huge No over Israel.
He walked off and left Shiloh empty,
 abandoned the shrine where he had met with
  Israel.
He let his pride and joy go to the dogs,
 turned his back on the pride of his life.
He turned them loose on fields of battle;
 angry, he let them fend for themselves.
Their young men went to war and never came back;
 their young women waited in vain.
Their priests were massacred,
 and their widows never shed a tear.

Suddenly the Lord was up on his feet
 like someone roused from deep sleep,
 shouting like a drunken warrior.
He hit his enemies hard, sent them running,
 yelping, not daring to look back.
He disqualified Joseph as leader,
 told Ephraim he didn't have what it takes,
And chose the Tribe of Judah instead,
 Mount Zion, which he loves so much.
He built his sanctuary there, resplendent,
 solid and lasting as the earth itself.
Then he chose David, his servant,
 handpicked him from his work in the sheep
  pens.

One day he was caring for the ewes and their lambs,
the next day God had him shepherding Jacob,
his people Israel, his prize possession.
His good heart made him a good shepherd;
he guided the people wisely and well.

79

An Asaph psalm

God! Barbarians have broken into your home,
violated your holy temple,
left Jerusalem a pile of rubble!
They've served up the corpses of your servants
as carrion food for birds of prey,
Threw the bones of your holy people
out to the wild animals to gnaw on.
They dumped out their blood
like buckets of water.
All around Jerusalem, their bodies
were left to rot, unburied.
We're nothing but a joke to our neighbors,
graffiti scrawled on the city walls.

How long do we have to put up with this, GOD?
Do you have it in for us for good?
Will your smoldering rage never cool down?
If you're going to be angry, be angry
with the pagans who care nothing about you,
or your rival kingdoms who ignore you.

They're the ones who ruined Jacob,
    who wrecked and looted the place where he
        lived.

Don't blame us for the sins of our parents.
    Hurry up and help us; we're at the end of our
        rope.
You're famous for helping; God, give *us* a break.
    Your reputation is on the line.
Pull us out of this mess, forgive us our sins—
    do what you're famous for doing!
Don't let the heathen get by with their sneers:
    "Where's your God? Is he out to lunch?"
Go public and show the godless world
    that they can't kill your servants and get by
        with it.

Give groaning prisoners a hearing;
    pardon those on death row from their doom—
        you can do it!
Give our jeering neighbors what they've got
        coming to them;
    let their God-taunts boomerang and knock
        them flat.
Then we, your people, the ones you love and care
        for,
    will thank you over and over and over.
We'll tell everyone we meet
    how wonderful you are, how praiseworthy you
        are!

80

An Asaph psalm

Listen, Shepherd, Israel's Shepherd—
    get all your Joseph sheep together.
Throw beams of light
    from your dazzling throne
So Ephraim, Benjamin, and Manasseh
    can see where they're going.
Get out of bed—you've slept long enough!
    Come on the run before it's too late.

    God, come back!
    Smile your blessing smile:
    That will be our salvation.

God, God-of-the-Angel-Armies,
    how long will you smolder like a sleeping volcano
    while your people call for fire and brimstone?
You put us on a diet of tears,
    bucket after bucket of salty tears to drink.
You make us look ridiculous to our friends;
    our enemies poke fun day after day.

    God-of-the-Angel Armies, come back!
    Smile your blessing smile:
    That will be our salvation.

Remember how you brought a young vine from
        Egypt,

cleared out the brambles and briers
  and planted your very own vineyard?
You prepared the good earth,
  you planted her roots deep;
  the vineyard filled the land.
Your vine soared high and shaded the mountains,
  even dwarfing the giant cedars.
Your vine ranged west to the Sea,
  east to the River.
So why do you no longer protect your vine?
  Trespassers pick its grapes at will;
Wild pigs crash through and crush it,
  and the mice nibble away at what's left.
God-of-the-Angel-Armies, turn our way!
  Take a good look at what's happened
  and attend to this vine.
Care for what you once tenderly planted—
  the vine you raised from a shoot.
And those who dared to set it on fire—
  give them a look that will kill!
Then take the hand of your once-favorite child,
  the child you raised to adulthood.
We will never turn our back on you;
  breathe life into our lungs so we can shout your
    name!

GOD, God-of-the-Angel-Armies, come back!
Smile your blessing smile:
That will be our salvation.

81

An Asaph psalm

A song to our strong God!
    a shout to the God of Jacob!
Anthems from the choir, music from the band,
    sweet sounds from lute and harp,
Trumpets and trombones and horns:
    it's festival day, a feast to God!
A day decreed by God,
    solemnly ordered by the God of Jacob.
He commanded Joseph to keep this day
    so we'd never forget what he did in Egypt.

    I hear this most gentle whisper from One
    I never guessed would speak to me:

"I took the world off your shoulders,
    freed you from a life of hard labor.
You called to me in your pain;
    I got you out of a bad place.
I answered you from where the thunder hides,
    I proved you at Meribah Fountain.

"Listen, dear ones—get this straight;
    oh Israel, don't take this lightly.
Don't take up with strange gods,
    don't worship the popular gods.

I'm GOD, your God, the very God
who rescued you from doom in Egypt,
Then fed you all you could eat,
filled your hungry stomachs.

"But my people didn't listen,
Israel paid no attention;
So I let go of the reins and told them, 'Run!
Do it your own way!'

"Oh, dear people, will you listen to me now?
Israel, will you follow my map?
I'll make short work of your enemies,
give your foes the back of my hand.
I'll send the GOD-haters cringing like dogs,
never to be heard from again.
You'll feast on my fresh-baked bread
spread with butter and rock-pure honey."

82

An Asaph psalm

God calls the judges into his courtroom,
he puts all the judges in the dock.

"Enough! You've corrupted justice long enough,
you've let the wicked get away with murder.
You're here to defend the defenseless,
to make sure that underdogs get a fair break;

Your job is to stand up for the powerless,
and prosecute all those who exploit them."

Ignorant judges! Head-in-the-sand judges!
They haven't a clue to what's going on.
And now everything's falling apart,
the world's coming unglued.

"I appointed you judges, each one of you,
deputies of the High God,
But you've betrayed your commission
and now you're stripped of your rank, busted."

O God, give them what they've got coming!
You've got the whole world in your hands!

83

An Asaph psalm

God, don't shut me out;
don't give me the silent treatment, O God.
Your enemies are out there whooping it up,
the God-haters are living it up;
They're plotting to do your people in,
conspiring to rob you of your precious ones.
"Let's wipe this nation from the face of the earth,"
they say; "scratch Israel's name off the books."
And now they're putting their heads together,
making plans to get rid of you.

Edom and the Ishmaelites,
Moab and the Hagrites,
Gebal and Ammon and Amalek,
Philistia and the Tyrians,
And now Assyria has joined up,
Giving muscle to the gang of Lot.

Do to them what you did to Midian,
to Sisera and Jabin at Kishon Brook;
They came to a bad end at Endor,
nothing but dung for the garden.
Cut down their leaders as you did Oreb and Zeeb,
their princes to nothings like Zebah and
Zalmunna,
With their empty brags, "We're grabbing it all,
grabbing God's gardens for ourselves."

My God! I've had it with them!
Blow them away!
Tumbleweeds in the desert waste,
charred sticks in the burned-over ground.
Knock the breath right out of them, so they're
gasping
for breath, gasping, "GOD."
Bring them to the end of their rope,
and leave them there dangling, helpless.
Then they'll learn your name: "GOD,"
the one and only High God on earth.

84

A Korah psalm

What a beautiful home, GOD-of-the-Angel-Armies!
I've always longed to live in a place like this,
Always dreamed of a room in your house,
where I could sing for joy to God-alive!

Birds find nooks and crannies in your house,
sparrows and swallows make nests there.
They lay their eggs and raise their young,
singing their songs in the place where we worship.
GOD-of-the-Angel-Armies! King! God!
How blessed they are to live and sing there!

And how blessed all those in whom you live,
whose lives become roads you travel;
They wind through lonesome valleys, come upon brooks,
discover cool springs and pools brimming with rain!
God-traveled, these roads curve up the mountain,
and at the last turn—Zion! God in full view!

God-of-the-Angel-Armies, listen:
O God of Jacob, open your ears—I'm praying!
Look at our shields, glistening in the sun,
our faces, shining with your gracious anointing.

One day spent in your house, this beautiful place
of worship,
beats thousands spent on Greek island beaches.
I'd rather scrub floors in the house of my God
than be honored as a guest in the palace of sin.
All sunshine and sovereign is GOD,
generous in gifts and glory.
He doesn't scrimp with his traveling companions.
It's smooth sailing all the way with GOD-of-
the-Angel Armies.

85

A KORAH PSALM

GOD, you smiled on your good earth!
You brought good times back to Jacob!
You lifted the cloud of guilt from your people,
you put their sins far out of sight.
You took back your sin-provoked threats,
you cooled your hot, righteous anger.

Help us again, God of our help;
don't hold a grudge against us forever.
You aren't going to keep this up, are you?
scowling and angry, year after year?
Why not help us make a fresh start—a resurrection
life?
Then your people will laugh and sing!
Show us how much you love us, GOD!
Give us the salvation we need!

I can't wait to hear what he'll say.
    GOD's about to pronounce his people well,
The holy people he loves so much,
    so they'll never again live like fools.
See how close his salvation is to those who fear him?
    Our country is home base for Glory!

Love and Truth meet in the street,
    Right Living and Whole Living embrace and kiss!
Truth sprouts green from the ground,
    Right Living pours down from the skies!
Oh yes! GOD gives Goodness and Beauty;
    our land responds with Bounty and Blessing.
Right Living strides out before him,
    and clears a path for his passage.

86

A David psalm

Bend an ear, GOD; answer me.
    I'm one miserable wretch!
Keep me safe—haven't I lived a good life?
    Help your servant—I'm depending on you!
You're my God; have mercy on me.
    I count on you from morning to night.
Give your servant a happy life;
    I put myself in your hands!
You're well-known as good and forgiving,
    bighearted to all who ask for help.

Pay attention, God, to my prayer;
bend down and listen to my cry for help.
Every time I'm in trouble I call on you,
confident that you'll answer.

There's no one quite like you among the gods,
O Lord,
and nothing to compare with your works.
All the nations you made are on their way,
ready to give honor to you, O Lord,
Ready to put your beauty on display,
parading your greatness,
And the great things you do—
God, you're the one, there's no one but you!

Train me, God, to walk straight;
then I'll follow your true path.
Put me together, one heart and mind;
then, undivided, I'll worship in joyful fear.
From the bottom of my heart I thank you, dear
Lord;
I've never kept secret what you're up to.
You've always been great toward me—what love!
You snatched me from the brink of disaster!
God, these bullies have reared their heads!
A gang of thugs is after me—
and they don't care a thing about you.
But you, O God, are both tender and kind,
not easily angered, immense in love,
and you never, never quit.

So look me in the eye and show kindness,
give your servant the strength to go on,
save your dear, dear child!
Make a show of how much you love me
so the bullies who hate me will stand there
slack-jawed,
As you, God, gently and powerfully
put me back on my feet.

87

A Korah psalm

He founded Zion on the Holy Mountain—
and oh, how God loves his home!
Loves it far better than all
the homes of Jacob put together!
God's hometown—oh!
everyone there is talking about you!

I name them off, those among whom I'm famous:
Egypt and Babylon,
also Philistia,
even Tyre, along with Cush.
Word's getting around; they point them out:
"This one was born again here!"

The word's getting out on Zion:
"Men and women, right and left,
get born again in her!"

GOD registers their names in his book:
"This one, this one, and this one—
born again, right here."

Singers and dancers give credit to Zion:
"All my springs are in you!"

88

A Korah prayer of Heman

GOD, you're my last chance of the day.
I spend the night on my knees before you.
Put me on your salvation agenda;
take notes on the trouble I'm in.
I've had my fill of trouble;
I'm camped on the edge of hell.
I'm written off as a lost cause,
one more statistic, a hopeless case.
Abandoned as already dead,
one more body in a stack of corpses,
And not so much as a gravestone—
I'm a black hole in oblivion.
You've dropped me into a bottomless pit,
sunk me in a pitch-black abyss.
I'm battered senseless by your rage,
relentlessly pounded by your waves of anger.
You turned my friends against me,
made me horrible to them.
I'm caught in a maze and can't find my way out,
blinded by tears of pain and frustration.

I call to you, God; all day I call.
  I wring my hands, I plead for help.
Are the dead a live audience for your miracles?
  Do ghosts ever join the choirs that praise you?
Does your love make any difference in a graveyard?
  Is your faithful presence noticed in the
    corridors of hell?
Are your marvelous wonders ever seen in the dark?
  your righteous ways noticed in the Land of No
    Memory?

I'm standing my ground, God, shouting for help,
  at my prayers every morning, on my knees each
    daybreak.
Why, God, do you turn a deaf ear?
  Why do you make yourself scarce?
For as long as I remember I've been hurting;
  I've taken the worst you can hand out, and I've
    had it.
Your wildfire anger has blazed through my life;
  I'm bleeding, black and blue.
You've attacked me fiercely from every side,
  raining down blows till I'm nearly dead.
You made lover and neighbor alike dump me;
  the only friend I have left is Darkness.

89

An Ethan prayer

Your love, God, is my song, and I'll sing it!
  I'm forever telling everyone how faithful you are.

I'll never quit telling the story of your love—
how you built the cosmos
and guaranteed everything in it.
Your love has always been our lives' foundation,
your fidelity has been the roof over our world.
You once said, "I joined forces with my chosen
leader,
I pledged my word to my servant, David, saying,
'Everyone descending from you is guaranteed life;
I'll make your rule as solid and lasting as rock.'"

GOD! Let the cosmos praise your wonderful
ways,
the choir of holy angels sing anthems to your
faithful ways!
Search high and low, scan skies and land,
you'll find nothing and no one quite like
GOD.
The holy angels are in awe before him;
he looms immense and august over everyone
around him.
GOD-of-the-Angel-Armies, who is like you,
powerful and faithful from every angle?
You put the arrogant ocean in its place
and calm its waves when they turn unruly.
You gave that old hag Egypt the back of your hand,
you brushed off your enemies with a flick of
your wrist.
You own the cosmos—you made everything in it,
everything from atom to archangel.

You positioned the North and South Poles;
the mountains Tabor and Hermon sing duets to
you.
With your well-muscled arm and your grip of
steel—
nobody messes with you!
The Right and Justice are the roots of your rule;
Love and Truth are its fruits.
Blessed are the people who know the passwords of
praise,
who shout on parade in the bright presence of
God.
Delighted, they dance all day long; they know
who you are, what you do—they can't keep it
quiet!
Your vibrant beauty has gotten inside us—
you've been so good to us! We're walking on air!
All we are and have we owe to God,
Holy God of Israel, our King!

A long time ago you spoke in a vision,
you spoke to your faithful beloved:
"I've crowned a hero,
I chose the best I could find;
I found David, my servant,
poured holy oil on his head,
And I'll keep my hand steadily on him,
yes, I'll stick with him through thick and thin.
No enemy will get the best of him,
no scoundrel will do him in.

I'll weed out all who oppose him,
I'll clean out all who hate him.
I'm with him for good and I'll love him forever;
I've set him on high—he's riding high!
I've put Ocean in his one hand, River in the other;
he'll call out, 'Oh, my Father—my God, my Rock of Salvation!'
Yes, I'm setting him apart as the First of the royal line,
High King over all of earth's kings.
I'll preserve him eternally in my love,
I'll faithfully do all I so solemnly promised.
I'll guarantee his family tree
and underwrite his rule.
If his children refuse to do what I tell them,
if they refuse to walk in the way I show them,
If they spit on the directions I give them
and tear up the rules I post for them—
I'll rub their faces in the dirt of their rebellion
and make them face the music.
But I'll never throw them out,
never abandon or disown them.
Do you think I'd withdraw my holy promise?
or take back words I'd already spoken?
I've given my word, my whole and holy word;
do you think I would lie to David?
His family tree is here for good,
his sovereignty as sure as the sun,
Dependable as the phases of the moon,
inescapable as weather."

But GOD, you did walk off and leave us,
you lost your temper with the one you anointed.
You tore up the promise you made to your servant,
you stomped his crown in the mud.
You blasted his home to kingdom come,
reduced his city to a pile of rubble
Picked clean by wayfaring strangers,
a joke to all the neighbors.
You declared a holiday for all his enemies,
and they're celebrating for all they're worth.
Angry, you opposed him in battle,
refused to fight on his side;
You robbed him of his splendor, humiliated this warrior,
ground his kingly honor in the dirt.
You took the best years of his life
and left him an impotent, ruined husk.
How long do we put up with this, GOD?
Are you gone for good? Will you hold this grudge forever?
Remember my sorrow and how short life is.
Did you create men and women for nothing but this?
We'll see death soon enough. Everyone does.
And there's no back door out of hell.
So where is the love you're so famous for, Lord?
What happened to your promise to David?
Take a good look at your servant, dear Lord;
I'm the butt of the jokes of all nations,

The taunting jokes of your enemies, God,
as they dog the steps of your dear anointed.

Blessed be God forever and always!
Yes. Oh, yes.

90

A prayer of Moses, man of God

God, it seems you've been our home forever;
long before the mountains were born,
Long before you brought earth itself to birth,
from "once upon a time" to "kingdom come"—
you are God.

So don't return us to mud, saying,
"Back to where you came from!"
Patience! You've got all the time in the world—
whether
a thousand years or a day, it's all the same to you.
Are we no more to you than a wispy dream,
no more than a blade of grass
That springs up gloriously with the rising sun
and is cut down without a second thought?
Your anger is far and away too much for us;
we're at the end of our rope.
You keep track of all our sins; every misdeed
since we were children is entered in your
books.

All we can remember is that frown on your face.
Is that all we're ever going to get?
We live for seventy years or so
(with luck we might make it to eighty),
And what do we have to show for it? Trouble.
Toil and trouble and a marker in the graveyard.
Who can make sense of such rage,
such anger against the very ones who fear you?

Oh! Teach us to live well!
Teach us to live wisely and well!
Come back, GOD—how long do we have to
wait?—
and treat your servants with kindness for a change.
Surprise us with love at daybreak;
then we'll skip and dance all the day long.
Make up for the bad times with some good times;
we've seen enough evil to last a lifetime.
Let your servants see what you're best at—
the ways you rule and bless your children.
And let the loveliness of our Lord, our God, rest
on us,
confirming the work that we do.
Oh, yes. Affirm the work that we do!

91

You who sit down in the High God's presence,
spend the night in Shaddai's shadow,

Say this: "GOD, you're my refuge.
I trust in you and I'm safe!"
That's right—he rescues you from hidden traps,
shields you from deadly hazards.
His huge outstretched arms protect you—
under them you're perfectly safe;
his arms fend off all harm.
Fear nothing—not wild wolves in the night,
not flying arrows in the day,
Not disease that prowls through the darkness,
not disaster that erupts at high noon.
Even though others succumb all around,
drop like flies right and left,
no harm will even graze you.
You'll stand untouched, watch it all from a distance,
watch the wicked turn into corpses.
Yes, because GOD's your refuge,
the High God your very own home,
Evil can't get close to you,
harm can't get through the door.
He ordered his angels
to guard you wherever you go.
If you stumble, they'll catch you;
their job is to keep you from falling.
You'll walk unharmed among lions and snakes,
and kick young lions and serpents from the path.

"If you'll hold on to me for dear life," says GOD,
"I'll get you out of any trouble.

I'll give you the best of care
    if you'll only get to know and trust me.
Call me and I'll answer, be at your side in bad times;
    I'll rescue you, then throw you a party.
I'll give you a long life,
    give you a long drink of salvation!"

92

A Sabbath song

What a beautiful thing, GOD, to give thanks,
    to sing an anthem to you, the High God!
To announce your love each daybreak,
    sing your faithful presence all through the night,
Accompanied by dulcimer and harp,
    the full-bodied music of strings.

You made me so happy, GOD.
    I saw your work and I shouted for joy.
How magnificent your work, GOD!
    How profound your thoughts!
Dullards never notice what you do;
    fools never do get it.
When the wicked popped up like weeds
    and all the evil men and women took over,
You mowed them down,
    finished them off once and for all.
You, GOD, are High and Eternal.
    Look at your enemies, GOD!

Look at your enemies—ruined!
Scattered to the winds, all those hirelings of evil!

But you've made me strong as a charging bison,
you've honored me with a festive parade.
The sight of my critics going down is still fresh,
the rout of my malicious detractors.
My ears are filled with the sounds of promise:
"Good people will prosper like palm trees,
Grow tall like Lebanon cedars;
transplanted to GOD's courtyard,
They'll grow tall in the presence of God,
lithe and green, virile still in old age."

Such witnesses to upright GOD!
My Mountain, my huge, holy Mountain!

93

GOD is King, robed and ruling,
GOD is robed and surging with strength.

And yes, the world is firm, immovable,
Your throne ever firm—you're Eternal!

Sea storms are up, GOD,
Sea storms wild and roaring,
Sea storms with thunderous breakers.

Stronger than wild sea storms,
Mightier than sea-storm breakers,
Mighty GOD rules from High Heaven.

What you say goes—it always has.
"Beauty" and "Holy" mark your palace rule,
GOD, to the very end of time.

94

GOD, put an end to evil;
avenging God, show your colors!
Judge of the earth, take your stand;
throw the book at the arrogant.

GOD, the wicked get away with murder—
how long will you let this go on?
They brag and boast
and crow about their crimes!

They walk all over your people, GOD,
exploit and abuse your precious people.
They take out anyone who gets in their way;
if they can't use them, they kill them.
They think, "GOD isn't looking,
Jacob's God is out to lunch."

Well, think again, you idiots,
fools—how long before you get smart?
Do you think Ear-Maker doesn't hear,
Eye-Shaper doesn't see?
Do you think the trainer of nations doesn't correct,
the teacher of Adam doesn't know?
GOD knows, all right—

knows your stupidity,
sees your shallowness.

How blessed the man you train, GOD,
the woman you instruct in your Word,
Providing a circle of quiet within the clamor of evil,
while a jail is being built for the wicked.
GOD will never walk away from his people,
never desert his precious people.
Rest assured that justice is on its way
and every good heart put right.

Who stood up for me against the wicked?
Who took my side against evil workers?
If GOD hadn't been there for me,
I never would have made it.
The minute I said, "I'm slipping, I'm falling,"
your love, GOD, took hold and held me fast.
When I was upset and beside myself,
you calmed me down and cheered me up.

Can Misrule have anything in common with you?
Can Troublemaker pretend to be on your side?
They ganged up on good people,
plotted behind the backs of the innocent.
But GOD became my hideout,
God was my high mountain retreat,
Then boomeranged their evil back on them:
for their evil ways he wiped them out,
our GOD cleaned them out for good.

95

Come, let's shout praises to GOD,
raise the roof for the Rock who saved us!
Let's march into his presence singing praises,
lifting the rafters with our hymns!

And why? Because GOD is the best,
High King over all the gods.
In one hand he holds deep caves and caverns,
in the other hand grasps the high mountains.
He made Ocean—he owns it!
His hands sculpted Earth!

So come, let us worship: bow before him,
on your knees before GOD, who made us!
Oh yes, he's our God,
and we're the people he pastures, the flock he feeds.

Drop everything and listen, listen as he speaks:
"Don't turn a deaf ear as in the Bitter Uprising,
As on the day of the Wilderness Test,
when your ancestors turned and put *me* to the test.
For forty years they watched me at work among them,
as over and over they tried my patience.
And I was provoked—oh, was I provoked!

'Can't they keep their minds on God for five
minutes?
Do they simply refuse to walk down my road?'
Exasperated, I exploded,
'They'll never get where they're headed,
never be able to sit down and rest.'"

96

Sing God a brand-new song!
Earth and everyone in it, sing!
Sing to God—*worship* God!

Shout the news of his victory from sea to sea,
Take the news of his glory to the lost,
News of his wonders to one and all!

For God is great, and worth a thousand
Hallelujahs.
His furious beauty puts the other gods to shame;
Pagan gods are mere tatters and rags.

God made the heavens—
Royal splendor radiates from him,
A powerful beauty sets him apart.

Bravo, God, Bravo!
Everyone join in the great shout: Encore!
In awe before the beauty, in awe before the might.

Bring gifts and celebrate,
Bow before the beauty of GOD,
Then to your knees—everyone worship!

Get out the message—GOD Rules!
He put the world on a firm foundation;
He treats everyone fair and square.

Let's hear it from Sky,
With Earth joining in,
And a huge round of applause from Sea.

Let Wilderness turn cartwheels,
Animals, come dance,
Put every tree of the forest in the choir—

An extravaganza before GOD as he comes,
As he comes to set everything right on earth,
Set everything right, treat everyone fair.

97

GOD rules: *there's* something to shout over!
On the double, mainlands and islands—celebrate!

Bright clouds and storm clouds circle 'round him;
Right and justice anchor his rule.

Fire blazes out before him,
Flaming high up the craggy mountains.

His lightnings light up the world;
Earth, wide-eyed, trembles in fear.

The mountains take one look at GOD
And melt, melt like wax before earth's Lord.

The heavens announce that he'll set everything
right,
And everyone will see it happen—glorious!

All who serve handcrafted gods will be sorry—
And they were so proud of their ragamuffin gods!

On your knees, all you gods—worship him!
And Zion, you listen and take heart!

Daughters of Zion, sing your hearts out:
GOD has done it all, has set everything right.

You, GOD, are High God of the cosmos,
Far, far higher than any of the gods.

GOD loves all who hate evil,
And those who love him he keeps safe,
Snatches them from the grip of the wicked.

Light-seeds are planted in the souls of God's people,
Joy-seeds are planted in good heart-soil.

So, God's people, shout praise to GOD,
Give thanks to our Holy God!

98

Sing to GOD a brand-new song.
He's made a world of wonders!

He rolled up his sleeves,
He set things right.

GOD made history with salvation,
He showed the world what he could do.

He remembered to love us, a bonus
To his dear family, Israel—indefatigable love.

The whole earth comes to attention.
Look—God's work of salvation!

Shout your praises to GOD, everybody!
Let loose and sing! Strike up the band!

Round up an orchestra to play for GOD,
Add on a hundred-voice choir.

Feature trumpets and big trombones,
Fill the air with praises to King GOD.

Let the sea and its fish give a round of applause,
With everything living on earth joining in.

Let ocean breakers call out, "Encore!"
And mountains harmonize the finale—

A tribute to GOD when he comes,
When he comes to set the earth right.

He'll straighten out the whole world,
He'll put the world right, and everyone in it.

99

GOD rules. On your toes, everybody!
He rules from his angel throne—take notice!
GOD looms majestic in Zion,
He towers in splendor over all the big names.
Great and terrible your beauty: let everyone praise you!
Holy. Yes, holy.

Strong King, lover of justice,
You laid things out fair and square;
You set down the foundations in Jacob,
Foundation stones of just and right ways.
Honor GOD, our God; worship his rule!
Holy. Yes, holy.

Moses and Aaron were his priests,
Samuel among those who prayed to him.
They prayed to GOD and he answered them;
He spoke from the pillar of cloud.
And they did what he said; they kept the law he gave them.
And then GOD, our God, answered them

(But you were never soft on their sins).
Lift high GOD, our God; worship at his holy
mountain.
Holy. Yes, holy is GOD our God.

100

A thanksgiving psalm

On your feet now—applaud GOD!
Bring a gift of laughter,
sing yourselves into his presence.

Know this: GOD is God, and God, GOD.
He made us; we didn't make him.
We're his people, his well-tended sheep.

Enter with the password: "Thank you!"
Make yourselves at home, talking praise.
Thank him. Worship him.

For GOD is sheer beauty,
all-generous in love,
loyal always and ever.

101

A David psalm

My theme song is God's love and justice,
and I'm singing it right to you, GOD.

I'm finding my way down the road of right living,
    but how long before you show up?
I'm doing the very best I can,
    and I'm doing it at home, where it counts.
I refuse to take a second look
    at corrupting people and degrading things.
I reject made-in-Canaan gods,
    stay clear of contamination.
The crooked in heart keep their distance;
    I refuse to shake hands with those who plan evil.
I put a gag on the gossip
    who bad-mouths his neighbor;
I can't stand
    arrogance.
But I have my eye on salt-of-the-earth people—
    they're the ones I want working with me;
Men and women on the straight and narrow—
    these are the ones I want at my side.
But no one who traffics in lies
    gets a job with me; I have no patience with liars.
I've rounded up all the wicked like cattle
    and herded them right out of the country.
I purged GOD's city
    of all who make a business of evil.

102

A prayer of one whose life is falling to pieces, and who lets GOD know just how bad it is

GOD, listen! Listen to my prayer,
    listen to the pain in my cries.

Don't turn your back on me
    just when I need you so desperately.
Pay attention! This is a cry for *help*!
    And hurry—this can't wait!

I'm wasting away to nothing,
    I'm burning up with fever.
I'm a ghost of my former self,
    half-consumed already by terminal illness.
My jaws ache from gritting my teeth;
    I'm nothing but skin and bones.
I'm like a buzzard in the desert,
    a crow perched on the rubble.
Insomniac, I twitter away,
    mournful as a sparrow in the gutter.
All day long my enemies taunt me,
    while others just curse.
They bring in meals—casseroles of ashes!
    I draw drink from a barrel of my tears.
And all because of your furious anger;
    you swept me up and threw me out.
There's nothing left of me—
    a withered weed, swept clean from the path.

Yet you, GOD, are sovereign still,
    always and ever sovereign.
You'll get up from your throne and help Zion—
    it's time for compassionate help.
Oh, how your servants love this city's rubble
    and weep with compassion over its dust!

The godless nations will sit up and take notice
—see your glory, worship your name—
When God rebuilds Zion,
when he shows up in all his glory,
When he attends to the prayer of the wretched.
He won't dismiss their prayer.

Write this down for the next generation
so people not yet born will praise God:
"God looked out from his high holy place;
from heaven he surveyed the earth.
He listened to the groans of the doomed,
he opened the doors of their death cells."
Write it so the story can be told in Zion,
so God's praise will be sung in Jerusalem's
streets
And wherever people gather together
along with their rulers to worship him.

God sovereignly brought me to my knees,
he cut me down in my prime.
"Oh, don't," I prayed, "please don't let me die.
You have more years than you know what to do
with!
You laid earth's foundations a long time ago,
and handcrafted the very heavens;
You'll still be around when they're long gone,
threadbare and discarded like an old suit of
clothes.
You'll throw them away like a worn-out coat,

but year after year you're as good as new.
Your servants' children will have a good place to
live
and their children will be at home with you."

103

A David psalm

Oh my soul, bless GOD.
From head to toe, I'll bless his holy name!
Oh my soul, bless GOD,
don't forget a single blessing!

He forgives your sins—every one.
He heals your diseases—every one.
He redeems you from hell—saves your life!
He crowns you with love and mercy—
a paradise crown.
He wraps you in goodness—beauty eternal.
He renews your youth—you're always young in
his presence.

GOD makes everything come out right;
he puts victims back on their feet.
He showed Moses how he went about his work,
opened up his plans to all Israel.
GOD is sheer mercy and grace;
not easily angered, he's rich in love.
He doesn't endlessly nag and scold,
nor hold grudges forever.

He doesn't treat us as our sins deserve,
nor pay us back in full for our wrongs.
As high as heaven is over the earth,
so strong is his love to those who fear him.
And as far as sunrise is from sunset,
he has separated us from our sins.
As parents feel for their children,
GOD feels for those who fear him.
He knows us inside and out,
keeps in mind that we're made of mud.
Men and women don't live very long;
like wildflowers they spring up and blossom,
But a storm snuffs them out just as quickly,
leaving nothing to show they were here.
GOD's love, though, is ever and always,
eternally present to all who fear him,
Making everything right for them and their children
as they follow his Covenant ways
and remember to do whatever he said.

GOD has set his throne in heaven;
he rules over us all. He's the King!
So bless GOD, you angels,
ready and able to fly at his bidding,
quick to hear and do what he says.
Bless GOD, all you armies of angels,
alert to respond to whatever he wills.
Bless GOD, all creatures, wherever you are—
everything and everyone made by GOD.

And you, oh my soul, bless GOD!

104

Oh my soul, bless GOD!

GOD, my God, how great you are!
 beautifully, gloriously robed,
Dressed up in sunshine,
 and all heaven stretched out for your tent.
You built your palace on the ocean deeps,
 made a chariot out of clouds and took off on
 wind-wings.
You commandeered winds as messengers,
 appointed fire and flame as ambassadors.
You set earth on a firm foundation
 so that nothing can shake it, ever.
You blanketed earth with ocean,
 covered the mountains with deep waters;
Then you roared and the water ran away—
 your thunder crash put it to flight.
Mountains pushed up, valleys spread out
 in the places you assigned them.
You set boundaries between earth and sea;
 never again will earth be flooded.
You started the springs and rivers,
 sent them flowing among the hills.
All the wild animals now drink their fill,
 wild donkeys quench their thirst.
Along the riverbanks the birds build nests,
 ravens make their voices heard.

You water the mountains from your heavenly
reservoirs;
earth is supplied with plenty of water.
You make grass grow for the livestock,
hay for the animals that plow the ground.

Oh yes, God brings grain from the land,
wine to make people happy,
Their faces glowing with health,
a people well-fed and hearty.
GOD's trees are well-watered—
the Lebanon cedars he planted.
Birds build their nests in those trees;
look—the stork at home in the treetop.
Mountain goats climb about the cliffs;
badgers burrow among the rocks.
The moon keeps track of the seasons,
the sun is in charge of each day.
When it's dark and night takes over,
all the forest creatures come out.
The young lions roar for their prey,
clamoring to God for their supper.
When the sun comes up, they vanish,
lazily stretched out in their dens.
Meanwhile, men and women go out to work,
busy at their jobs until evening.

What a wildly wonderful world, GOD!
You made it all, with Wisdom at your side,
made earth overflow with your wonderful creations.

Oh, look—the deep, wide sea,
    brimming with fish past counting,
    sardines and sharks and salmon.
Ships plow those waters,
    and Leviathan, your pet dragon, romps in them.
All the creatures look expectantly to you
    to give them their meals on time.
You come, and they gather around;
    you open your hand and they eat from it.
If you turned your back,
    they'd die in a minute—
Take back your Spirit and they die,
    revert to original mud;
Send out your Spirit and they spring to life—
    the whole countryside in bloom and blossom.

The glory of GOD—let it last forever!
    Let GOD enjoy his creation!
He takes one look at earth and triggers an earthquake,
    points a finger at the mountains, and volcanoes
        erupt.

Oh, let me sing to GOD all my life long,
    sing hymns to my God as long as I live!
Oh, let my song please him;
    I'm so pleased to be singing to GOD.
But clear the ground of sinners—
    no more godless men and women!

Oh my soul, bless GOD!

105

Hallelujah!

Thank GOD! Pray to him by name!
    Tell everyone you meet what he has done!
Sing him songs, belt out hymns,
    translate his wonders into music!
Honor his holy name with Hallelujahs,
    you who seek GOD. Live a happy life!
Keep your eyes open for GOD, watch for his
        works;
    be alert for signs of his presence.
Remember the world of wonders he has made,
    his miracles, and the verdicts he's rendered—
        Oh seed of Abraham, his servant,
        Oh child of Jacob, his chosen.

He's GOD, our God,
    in charge of the whole earth.
And he remembers, remembers his Covenant—
    for a thousand generations he's been as good as
        his word.
It's the Covenant he made with Abraham,
    the same oath he swore to Isaac,
The very statute he established with Jacob,
    the eternal Covenant with Israel,
Namely, "I give you the land.
    Canaan is your hill-country inheritance."

When they didn't count for much,
a mere handful, and strangers at that,
Wandering from country to country,
drifting from pillar to post,
He permitted no one to abuse them.
He told kings to keep their hands off:
"Don't you dare lay a hand on my anointed,
don't hurt a hair on the heads of my prophets."

Then he called down a famine on the country,
he broke every last blade of wheat.
But he sent a man on ahead:
Joseph, sold as a slave.
They put cruel chains on his ankles,
an iron collar around his neck,
Until God's word came to the Pharaoh,
and GOD confirmed his promise.
God sent the king to release him.
The Pharaoh set Joseph free;
He appointed him master of his palace,
put him in charge of all his business
To personally instruct his princes
and train his advisors in wisdom.

Then Israel entered Egypt,
Jacob immigrated to Africa.
God gave his people lots of babies;
soon their numbers alarmed their foes.
He turned the Egyptians against his people;
they abused and cheated God's servants.

Then he sent his servant Moses,
    and Aaron, whom he also chose.
They worked marvels in that spiritual wasteland,
    miracles in the Land of Ham.
He spoke, "Darkness!" and it turned dark—
    they couldn't see what they were doing.
He turned all their water to blood
    so that all their fish died;
He made frogs swarm through the land,
    even into the king's bedroom;
He gave the word and flies swarmed,
    gnats filled the air.
He substituted hail for rain,
    he stabbed their land with lightning;
He wasted their vines and fig trees,
    smashed their groves of trees to splinters;
With a word he brought in locusts,
    millions of locusts, armies of locusts;
They consumed every blade of grass in the country
    and picked the ground clean of produce;
He struck down every firstborn in the land,
    the first fruits of their virile powers.
He led Israel out, their arms filled with loot,
    and not one among his tribes even stumbled.
Egypt was glad to have them go—
    they were scared to death of them.
God spread a cloud to keep them cool through the day
    and a fire to light their way through the night;
They prayed and he brought quail,

filled them with the bread of heaven;
He opened the rock and water poured out;
it flowed like a river through that desert—
All because he remembered his Covenant,
his promise to Abraham, his servant.

Remember this! He led his people out singing for joy;
his chosen people marched, singing their hearts out!
He made them a gift of the country they entered,
helped them seize the wealth of the nations
So they could do everything he told them—
could follow his instructions to the letter.

Hallelujah!

106

Hallelujah!
Thank GOD! And why?
Because he's good, because his love lasts.
But who on earth can do it—
declaim GOD's mighty acts, broadcast all his praises?
You're one happy man when you do what's right,
one happy woman when you form the habit of justice.

Remember me, GOD, when you enjoy your people;

include me when you save them;
I want to see your chosen succeed,
celebrate with your celebrating nation,
join the Hallelujahs of your pride and joy!

We've sinned a lot, both we and our parents;
We've fallen short, hurt a lot of people.
After our parents left Egypt,
they took your wonders for granted,
forgot your great and wonderful love.
They were barely beyond the Red Sea
when they defied the High God
—the very place he saved them!
—the place he revealed his amazing power!
He rebuked the Red Sea so that it dried up on the
spot
—he paraded them right through!
—no one so much as got wet feet!
He saved them from a life of oppression,
pried them loose from the grip of the enemy.
Then the waters flowed back on their oppressors;
there wasn't a single survivor.
Then they believed his words were true
and broke out in songs of praise.

But it wasn't long before they forgot the whole thing,
wouldn't wait to be told what to do.
They only cared about pleasing themselves in that
desert,
provoked God with their insistent demands.

He gave them exactly what they asked for—
    but along with it they got an empty heart.
One day in camp some grew jealous of Moses,
    also of Aaron, holy priest of God.
The ground opened and swallowed Dathan,
    then buried Abiram's gang.
Fire flared against that rebel crew
    and torched them to a cinder.

They cast in metal a bull calf at Horeb
    and worshiped the statue they'd made.
They traded the Glory
    for a cheap piece of sculpture—a grass-chewing
        bull!
They forgot God, their very own Savior,
    who turned things around in Egypt,
Who created a world of wonders in Africa,
    who gave that stunning performance at the Red
        Sea.

Fed up, God decided to get rid of them—
    and except for Moses, his chosen, he would have.
But Moses stood in the gap and deflected God's anger,
    prevented it from destroying them utterly.
They went on to reject the Blessed Land,
    didn't believe a word of what God promised.
They found fault with the life they had
    and turned a deaf ear to God's voice.

Exasperated, God swore
that he'd lay them low in the desert,
Scattering their children here and there,
strewing them all over the earth.

Then they linked up with Baal Peor,
attending funeral banquets and eating idol food.
That made God so angry
that a plague spread through their ranks;
Phinehas stood up and pled their case
and the plague was stopped.
This was counted to his credit;
his descendants will never forget it.

They angered God again at Meribah Springs;
this time Moses got mixed up in their evil;
Because they defied God yet again,
Moses exploded and lost his temper.

They didn't wipe out those godless cultures
as ordered by God;
Instead they intermarried with the heathen,
and in time became just like them.
They worshiped their idols,
were caught in the trap of idols.
They sacrificed their sons and daughters
at the altars of demon gods.
They slit the throats of their babies,
murdered their infant girls and boys.
They offered their babies to Canaan's gods;
the blood of their babies stained the land.

Their way of life reeked;
they lived like prostitutes.

And God was furious—a wildfire anger;
he couldn't stand even to look at his people.
He turned them over to the heathen
so that the people who hated them ruled them.
Their enemies made life hard for them;
they were tyrannized under that rule.
Over and over God rescued them, but they never
learned—
until finally their sins destroyed them.

Still, when God saw the trouble they were in
and heard their cries for help,
He remembered his Covenant with them,
and, immense with love, took them by the hand.
He poured out his mercy on them
while their captors looked on, amazed.

Save us, God, our God!
Gather us back out of exile
So we can give thanks to your holy name
and join in the glory when you are praised!

Blessed be God, Israel's God!
Bless now, bless always!
Oh! Let everyone say Amen!
Hallelujah!

107

Oh, thank GOD—he's so good!
His love never runs out.
All of you set free by GOD, tell the world!
Tell how he freed you from oppression,
Then rounded you up from all over the place,
from the four winds, from the seven seas.

Some of you wandered for years in the desert,
looking but not finding a good place to live,
Half-starved and parched with thirst,
staggering and stumbling, on the brink of
exhaustion.
Then, in your desperate condition, you called out
to GOD.
He got you out in the nick of time;
He put your feet on a wonderful road
that took you straight to a good place to live.
So thank GOD for his marvelous love,
for his miracle mercy to the children he loves.
He poured great drafts of water down parched
throats;
the starved and hungry got plenty to eat.

Some of you were locked in a dark cell,
cruelly confined behind bars,
Punished for defying God's Word,
for turning your back on the High God's counsel—

A hard sentence, and your hearts so heavy,
and not a soul in sight to help.
Then you called out to GOD in your desperate condition;
he got you out in the nick of time.
He led you out of your dark, dark cell,
broke open the jail and led you out.
So thank GOD for his marvelous love,
for his miracle mercy to the children he loves;
He shattered the heavy jailhouse doors,
he snapped the prison bars like matchsticks!

Some of you were sick because you'd lived a bad life,
your bodies feeling the effects of your sin;
You couldn't stand the sight of food,
so miserable you thought you'd be better off dead.
Then you called out to GOD in your desperate condition;
he got you out in the nick of time.
He spoke the word that healed you,
that pulled you back from the brink of death.
So thank GOD for his marvelous love,
for his miracle mercy to the children he loves;
Offer thanksgiving sacrifices,
tell the world what he's done—sing it out!

Some of you set sail in big ships;
you put to sea to do business in faraway ports.
Out at sea you saw GOD in action,
saw his breathtaking ways with the ocean:

With a word he called up the wind—
an ocean storm, towering waves!
You shot high in the sky, then the bottom dropped out;
your hearts were stuck in your throats.
You were spun like a top, you reeled like a drunk,
you didn't know which end was up.
Then you called out to God in your desperate condition;
he got you out in the nick of time.
He quieted the wind down to a whisper,
put a muzzle on all the big waves.
And you were so glad when the storm died down,
and he led you safely back to harbor.
So thank God for his marvelous love,
for his miracle mercy to the children he loves.
Lift high your praises when the people assemble,
shout Hallelujah when the elders meet!

God turned rivers into wasteland,
springs of water into sunbaked mud;
Luscious orchards became alkali flats
because of the evil of the people who lived there.
Then he changed wasteland into fresh pools of water,
arid earth into springs of water,
Brought in the hungry and settled them there;
they moved in—what a great place to live!
They sowed the fields, they planted vineyards,
they reaped a bountiful harvest.

He blessed them and they prospered greatly;
their herds of cattle never decreased.
But abuse and evil and trouble declined
as he heaped scorn on princes and sent them away.
He gave the poor a safe place to live,
treated their clans like well-cared-for sheep.

Good people see this and are glad;
bad people are speechless, stopped in their tracks.
If you are really wise, you'll think this over—
it's time you appreciated GOD's deep love.

108

A David prayer

I'm ready, God, so ready,
ready from head to toe.
Ready to sing,
ready to raise a God-song:
"Wake, soul! Wake, lute!
Wake up, you sleepyhead sun!"

I'm thanking you, GOD, out in the streets,
singing your praises in town and country.
The deeper your love, the higher it goes;
every cloud's a flag to your faithfulness.
Soar high in the skies, O God!
Cover the whole earth with your glory!

And for the sake of the one you love so much,
reach down and help me—answer me!

That's when God spoke in holy splendor:
"Brimming over with joy,
I make a present of Shechem,
I hand out Succoth Valley as a gift.
Gilead's in my pocket,
to say nothing of Manasseh.
Ephraim's my hard hat,
Judah my hammer.
Moab's a scrub bucket—
I mop the floor with Moab,
Spit on Edom,
rain fireworks all over Philistia."

Who will take me to the thick of the fight?
Who'll show me the road to Edom?
You aren't giving up on us, are you, God?
refusing to go out with our troops?

Give us help for the hard task;
human help is worthless.
In God we'll do our very best;
he'll flatten the opposition for good.

109

A David prayer

My God, don't turn a deaf ear to my hallelujah prayer.
Liars are pouring out invective on me;

Their lying tongues are like a pack of dogs out to
get me,
barking their hate, nipping my heels—and for
no reason!
I loved them and now they slander me—yes, me!—
and treat my prayer like a crime;
They return my good with evil,
they return my love with hate.

Send the Evil One to accuse my accusing judge;
dispatch Satan to prosecute him.
When he's judged, let the verdict be, "Guilty,"
and when he prays, let his prayer turn to sin.
Give him a short life,
and give his job to somebody else.
Make orphans of his children,
dress his wife in widow's black;
Turn his children into begging street urchins,
evicted from their homes—homeless.
May the bank foreclose and wipe him out,
and strangers, like vultures, pick him clean.
May there be no one around to help him out,
no one willing to give his orphans a break.
Chop down his family tree
so that nobody even remembers his name.
But erect a memorial to the sin of his father,
and make sure his mother's name is there, too—
Their sins recorded forever before GOD,
but they themselves sunk in oblivion.
That's all he deserves since he was never once kind,

hounded the afflicted and heartbroken to their
graves.
Since he loved cursing so much,
let curses rain down;
Since he had no taste for blessing,
let blessings flee far from him.
He dressed up in curses like a fine suit of clothes;
he drank curses, took his baths in curses.
So give him a gift—a costume of curses;
he can wear curses every day of the week!
That's what they'll get, those out to get me—
an avalanche of just deserts from GOD.

Oh, GOD, my Lord, step in;
work a miracle for me—you can do it!
Get me out of here—your love is so great!—
I'm at the end of my rope, my life in ruins.
I'm fading away to nothing, passing away,
my youth gone, old before my time.
I'm weak from hunger and can hardly stand up,
my body a rack of skin and bones.
I'm a joke in poor taste to those who see me;
they take one look and shake their heads.

Help me, oh help me, GOD, my God,
save me through your wonderful love;
Then they'll know that your hand is in this,
that you, GOD, have been at work.
Let them curse all they want;
you do the blessing.

Let them be jeered by the crowd when they stand up,
followed by cheers for me, your servant.
Dress my accusers in clothes dirty with shame,
discarded and humiliating old ragbag clothes.

My mouth's full of great praise for GOD,
I'm singing his hallelujahs surrounded by crowds,
For he's always at hand to take the side of the needy,
to rescue a life from the unjust judge.

110

A David prayer

The word of GOD to my Lord:
"Sit alongside me here on my throne
until I make your enemies a stool for your feet."
You were forged a strong scepter by GOD of Zion;
now rule, though surrounded by enemies!
Your people will freely join you, resplendent in
holy armor
on the great day of your conquest,
Join you at the fresh break of day,
join you with all the vigor of youth.

GOD gave his word and he won't take it back:
you're the permanent priest, the Melchizedek
priest.
The Lord stands true at your side,
crushing kings in his terrible wrath,

Bringing judgment on the nations,
    handing out convictions wholesale,
    crushing opposition across the wide earth.
The King-Maker put his King on the throne;
    the True King rules with head held high!

111

Hallelujah!
I give thanks to God with everything I've got—
Wherever good people gather, and in the
        congregation.
God's works are so great, worth
A lifetime of study—endless enjoyment!
Splendor and beauty mark his craft;
His generosity never gives out.
His miracles are his memorial—
This God of Grace, this God of Love.
He gave food to those who fear him,
He remembered to keep his ancient promise.
He proved to his people that he could do what he
        said:
Hand them the nations on a platter—a gift!
He manufactures truth and justice;
All his products are guaranteed to last—
Never out-of-date, never obsolete, rust-proof.
All that he makes and does is honest and true:
He paid the ransom for his people,
He ordered his Covenant kept forever.
He's so personal and holy, worthy of our respect.

The good life begins in the fear of GOD—
Do that and you'll know the blessing of GOD.
His Hallelujah lasts forever!

112

Hallelujah!
Blessed man, blessed woman, who fear GOD,
Who cherish and relish his commandments,
Their children robust on the earth,
And the homes of the upright—how blessed!
Their houses brim with wealth
And a generosity that never runs dry.
Sunrise breaks through the darkness for good
    people—
God's grace and mercy and justice!
The good person is generous and lends lavishly;
No shuffling or stumbling around for this one,
But a sterling and solid and lasting reputation.
Unfazed by rumor and gossip,
Heart ready, trusting in GOD,
Spirit firm, unperturbed,
Ever blessed, relaxed among enemies,
They lavish gifts on the poor—
A generosity that goes on, and on, and on.
An honored life! A beautiful life!
Someone wicked takes one look and rages,
Blusters away but ends up speechless.
There's nothing to the dreams of the wicked.
    Nothing.

113

Hallelujah!
You who serve GOD, praise GOD!
    Just to speak his name is praise!
Just to remember GOD is a blessing—
    now and tomorrow and always.
From east to west, from dawn to dusk,
    keep lifting all your praises to GOD!

GOD is higher than anything and anyone,
    outshining everything you can see in the skies.
Who can compare with GOD, our God,
    so majestically enthroned,
Surveying his magnificent
    heavens and earth?
He picks up the poor from out of the dirt,
    rescues the forgotten who've been thrown out
        with the trash,
Seats them among the honored guests,
    a place of honor among the brightest and best.
He gives childless couples a family,
    gives them joy as the parents of children.
Hallelujah!

114

After Israel left Egypt,
    the clan of Jacob left those barbarians behind;

Judah became holy land for him,
    Israel the place of holy rule.
Sea took one look and ran the other way;
    River Jordan turned around and ran off.
The mountains turned playful and skipped like
        rams,
    the hills frolicked like spring lambs.
What's wrong with you, Sea, that you ran away?
    and you, River Jordan, that you turned and ran
        off?
And mountains, why did you skip like rams?
    and you, hills, frolic like spring lambs?
Tremble, Earth! You're in the Lord's presence!
    in the presence of Jacob's God.
He turned the rock into a pool of cool water,
    turned flint into fresh spring water.

115

Not for our sake, GOD, no, not for our sake,
    but for your name's sake, show your glory.
Do it on account of your merciful love,
    do it on account of your faithful ways.
Do it so none of the nations can say,
    "Where now, oh where is their God?"

Our God is in heaven
    doing whatever he wants to do.
Their gods are metal and wood,
    handmade in a basement shop:

Carved mouths that can't talk,
painted eyes that can't see,
Tin ears that can't hear,
molded noses that can't smell,
Hands that can't grasp, feet that can't walk or run,
throats that never utter a sound.
Those who make them have become just like them,
have become just like the gods they trust.

But you, Israel: put your trust in GOD!
—trust your Helper! trust your Ruler!
Clan of Aaron, trust in GOD!
—trust your Helper! trust your Ruler!
You who fear GOD, trust in GOD!
—trust your Helper! trust your Ruler!

O GOD, remember us and bless us,
bless the families of Israel and Aaron.
And let GOD bless all who fear GOD—
bless the small, bless the great.
Oh, let GOD enlarge your families—
giving growth to you, growth to your children.
May you be blessed by GOD,
by GOD, who made heaven and earth.
The heaven of heavens is for GOD,
but he put us in charge of the earth.

Dead people can't praise GOD—
not a word to be heard from those buried in the ground.

But we bless GOD, oh yes—
    we bless him now, we bless him always!
Hallelujah!

116

I love GOD because he listened to me,
    listened as I begged for mercy.
He listened so intently
    as I laid out my case before him.
Death stared me in the face,
    hell was hard on my heels.
Up against it, I didn't know which way to turn;
    then I called out to GOD for help:
"Please, GOD!" I cried out.
    "Save my life!"
GOD is gracious—it is he who makes things
        right,
    our most compassionate God.
GOD takes the side of the helpless;
    when I was at the end of my rope, he saved me.

    I said to myself, "Relax and rest.
    GOD has showered you with blessings.
    Soul, you've been rescued from death;
    Eye, you've been rescued from tears;
    And you, Foot, were kept from stumbling."

I'm striding in the presence of GOD,
    alive in the land of the living!

I stayed faithful, though overwhelmed,
and despite a ton of bad luck,
Despite giving up on the human race,
saying, "They're all liars and cheats."

What can I give back to GOD
for the blessings he's poured out on me?
I'll lift high the cup of salvation—a toast to GOD!
I'll pray in the name of GOD;
I'll complete what I promised GOD I'd do,
and I'll do it together with his people.
When they arrive at the gates of death,
GOD welcomes those who love him.
Oh, GOD, here I am, your servant,
your faithful servant: set me free for your service!
I'm ready to offer the thanksgiving sacrifice
and pray in the name of GOD.
I'll complete what I promised GOD I'd do,
and I'll do it in company with his people,
In the place of worship, in GOD's house,
in Jerusalem, GOD's city.
Hallelujah!

117

Praise GOD, everybody!
Applaud GOD, all people!
His love has taken over our lives;
GOD's faithful ways are eternal.
Hallelujah!

118

Thank GOD because he's good,
because his love never quits.
Tell the world, Israel,
"His love never quits."
And you, clan of Aaron, tell the world,
"His love never quits."
And you who fear GOD, join in,
"His love never quits."

Pushed to the wall, I called to GOD;
from the wide open spaces, he answered.
GOD's now at my side and I'm not afraid;
who would dare lay a hand on me?
GOD's my strong champion;
I flick off my enemies like flies.
Far better to take refuge in GOD
than trust in people;
Far better to take refuge in GOD
than trust in celebrities.
Hemmed in by barbarians,
in GOD's name I rubbed their faces in the dirt;
Hemmed in and with no way out,
in GOD's name I rubbed their faces in the dirt;
Like swarming bees, like wild prairie fire, they
hemmed me in;
in GOD's name I rubbed their faces in the dirt.
I was right on the cliff-edge, ready to fall,
when GOD grabbed and held me.

GOD's my strength, he's also my song,
and now he's my salvation.
Hear the shouts, hear the triumph songs
in the camp of the saved?
"The hand of GOD has turned the tide!
The hand of GOD is raised in victory!
The hand of GOD has turned the tide!"

I didn't die. I *lived*!
And now I'm telling the world what GOD did.
GOD tested me, he pushed me hard,
but he didn't hand me over to Death.
Swing wide the city gates—the *righteous* gates!
I'll walk right through and thank GOD!
This Temple Gate belongs to GOD,
so the victors can enter and praise.

Thank you for responding to me;
you've truly become my salvation!
The stone the masons discarded as flawed
is now the capstone!
This is GOD's work.
We rub our eyes—we can hardly believe it!
This is the very day GOD acted—
let's celebrate and be festive!
Salvation now, GOD. Salvation now!
Oh yes, GOD—a free and full life!

Blessed are you who enter in GOD's name—
from GOD's house we bless you!

GOD is God,
he has bathed us in light.
Adorn the shrine with garlands,
hang colored banners above the altar!
You're my God, and I thank you.
Oh my God, I lift high your praise.
Thank GOD—he's so good.
His love never quits!

119

You're blessed when you stay on course,
walking steadily on the road revealed by GOD.
You're blessed when you follow his directions,
doing your best to find him.
That's right—you don't go off on your own;
you walk straight along the road he set.
You, GOD, prescribed the right way to live;
now you expect us to live it.
Oh, that my steps might be steady,
keeping to the course you set;
Then I'd never have any regrets
in comparing my life with your counsel.
I thank you for speaking straight from your heart;
I learn the pattern of your righteous ways.
I'm going to do what you tell me to do;
don't ever walk off and leave me.

How can a young person live a clean life?
By carefully reading the map of your Word.
I'm single-minded in pursuit of you;
don't let me miss the road signs you've posted.
I've banked your promises in the vault of my heart
so I won't sin myself bankrupt.
Be blessed, God;
train me in your ways of wise living.
I'll transfer to my lips
all the counsel that comes from your mouth;
I delight far more in what you tell me about living
than in gathering a pile of riches.
I ponder every morsel of wisdom from you,
I attentively watch how you've done it.
I relish everything you've told me of life,
I won't forget a word of it.

Be generous with me and I'll live a full life;
not for a minute will I take my eyes off your road.
Open my eyes so I can see
what you show me of your miracle-wonders.
I'm a stranger in these parts;
give me clear directions.
My soul is starved and hungry, ravenous!—
insatiable for your nourishing commands.
And those who think they know so much,
ignoring everything you tell them—let them
have it!

Don't let them mock and humiliate me;
I've been careful to do just what you said.
While bad neighbors maliciously gossip about me,
I'm absorbed in pondering your wise counsel.
Yes, your sayings on life are what give me delight;
I listen to them as to good neighbors!

I'm feeling terrible—I couldn't feel worse!
Get me on my feet again. You promised,
remember?
When I told my story, you responded;
train me well in your deep wisdom.
Help me understand these things inside and out
so I can ponder your miracle-wonders.
My sad life's dilapidated, a falling-down barn;
build me up again by your Word.
Barricade the road that goes Nowhere;
grace me with your clear revelation.
I choose the true road to Somewhere,
I post your road signs at every curve and corner.
I grasp and cling to whatever you tell me;
GOD, don't let me down!
I'll run the course you lay out for me
if you'll just show me how.

GOD, teach me lessons for living
so I can stay the course.

Give me insight so I can do what you tell me—
    my whole life one long, obedient response.
Guide me down the road of your commandments;
    I love traveling this freeway!
Give me an appetite for your words of wisdom,
    and not for piling up loot.
Divert my eyes from toys and trinkets,
    invigorate me on the pilgrim way.
Affirm your promises to me—
    promises made to all who fear you.
Deflect the harsh words of my critics—
    but what you say is always so good.
See how hungry I am for your counsel;
    preserve my life through your righteous ways!

Let your love, GOD, shape my life
    with salvation, exactly as you promised;
Then I'll be able to stand up to mockery
    because I trusted your Word.
Don't ever deprive me of truth, not ever—
    your commandments are what I depend on.
Oh, I'll guard with my life what you've revealed
        to me,
    guard it now, guard it ever;
And I'll stride freely through wide open spaces
    as I look for your truth and your wisdom;
Then I'll tell the world what I find,
    speak out boldly in public, unembarrassed.

I cherish your commandments—oh, how I love
them!—
relishing every fragment of your counsel.

Remember what you said to me, your servant—
I hang on to these words for dear life!
These words hold me up in bad times;
yes, your promises rejuvenate me.
The haters hate me without mercy,
but I don't budge from your revelation.
I watch for your ancient landmark words,
and know I'm on the right track.
But when I see the wicked ignore your directions,
I'm beside myself with anger.
I set your instructions to music
and sing them as I walk this pilgrim way.
I meditate on your name all night, GOD,
treasuring your revelation, O GOD.
Still, I walk through a rain of derision
because I live by your Word and counsel.

Because you have satisfied me, GOD, I promise
to do everything you say.
I beg you from the bottom of my heart: smile,
be gracious to me just as you promised.
When I took a long, careful look at your ways,
I got my feet back on the trail you blazed.

I was up at once, didn't drag my feet,
was quick to follow your orders.
The wicked hemmed me in—there was no way out—
but not for a minute did I forget your plan for me.
I get up in the middle of the night to thank you;
your decisions are so right, so true—I can't wait
till morning!
I'm a friend and companion of all who fear you,
of those committed to living by your rules.
Your love, GOD, fills the earth!
Train me to live by your counsel.

Be good to your servant, GOD;
be as good as your Word.
Train me in good common sense;
I'm thoroughly committed to living your way.
Before I learned to answer you, I wandered all over
the place,
but now I'm in step with your Word.
You are good, and the source of good;
train me in your goodness.
The godless spread lies about me,
but I focus my attention on what you are
saying;
They're bland as a bucket of lard,
while I dance to the tune of your revelation.
My troubles turned out all for the best—
they forced me to learn from your textbook.

Truth from your mouth means more to me
than striking it rich in a gold mine.

With your very own hands you formed me;
now breathe your wisdom over me so I can
understand you.
When they see me waiting, expecting your Word,
those who fear you will take heart and be glad.
I can see now, GOD, that your decisions are right;
your testing has taught me what's true and right.
Oh, love me—and right now!—hold me tight!
just the way you promised.
Now comfort me so I can live, really live;
your revelation is the tune I dance to.
Let the fast-talking tricksters be exposed as frauds;
they tried to sell me a bill of goods,
but I kept my mind fixed on your counsel.
Let those who fear you turn to me
for evidence of your wise guidance.
And let me live whole and holy, soul and body,
so I can always walk with my head held high.

I'm homesick—longing for your salvation;
I'm waiting for your word of hope.
My eyes grow heavy watching for some sign of
your promise;
how long must I wait for your comfort?

There's smoke in my eyes—they burn and water,
but I keep a steady gaze on the instructions you post.
How long do I have to put up with all this?
How long till you haul my tormentors into court?
The arrogant godless try to throw me off track,
ignorant as they are of God and his ways.
Everything you command is a sure thing,
but they harass me with lies. Help!
They've pushed and pushed—they never let up—
but I haven't relaxed my grip on your counsel.
In your great love revive me
so I can alertly obey your every word.

What you say goes, GOD,
and *stays*, as permanent as the heavens.
Your truth never goes out of fashion;
it's as relevant as the earth when the sun comes up.
Your Word and truth are dependable as ever;
that's what you ordered—you set the earth going.
If your revelation hadn't delighted me so,
I would have given up when the hard times came.
But I'll never forget the advice you gave me;
you saved my life with those wise words.
Save me! I'm all yours.
I look high and low for your words of wisdom.

The wicked lie in ambush to destroy me,
but I'm only concerned with your plans for me.
I see the limits to everything human,
but the horizons can't contain your commands!

Oh, how I love all you've revealed;
I reverently ponder it all the day long.
Your commands give me an edge on my enemies;
they never become obsolete.
I've even become smarter than my teachers
since I've pondered and absorbed your counsel.
I've become wiser than the wise old sages
simply by doing what you tell me.
I watch my step, avoiding the ditches and ruts of evil
so I can spend all my time keeping your Word.
I never make detours from the route you laid out;
you gave me such good directions.
Your words are so choice, so tasty;
I prefer them to the best home cooking.
With your instruction, I understand life;
that's why I hate false propaganda.

By your words I can see where I'm going;
they throw a beam of light on my dark path.
I've committed myself and I'll never turn back
from living by your righteous order.

Everything's falling apart on me, GOD;
put me together again with your Word.
Adorn me with your finest sayings, GOD;
teach me your holy rules.
My life is as close as my own hands,
but I don't forget what you have revealed.
The wicked do their best to throw me off track,
but I don't swerve an inch from your course.
I inherited your book on living; it's mine forever—
what a gift! And how happy it makes me!
I concentrate on doing exactly what you say—
I always have and always will.

I hate the two-faced,
but I love your clear-cut revelation.
You're my place of quiet retreat;
I wait for your Word to renew me.
Get out of my life, evildoers,
so I can keep my God's commands.
Take my side as you promised; I'll live then for sure.
Don't disappoint all my grand hopes.
Stick with me and I'll be all right;
I'll give total allegiance to your definitions of life.
Expose all who drift away from your sayings;
their casual idolatry is lethal.
You reject earth's wicked as so much rubbish;
therefore I lovingly embrace everything you say.

I shiver in awe before you;
your decisions leave me speechless with reverence.

I stood up for justice and the right;
don't leave me to the mercy of my oppressors.
Take the side of your servant, good God;
don't let the godless take advantage of me.
I can't keep my eyes open any longer, waiting for you
to keep your promise to set everything right.
Let your love dictate how you deal with me;
teach me from your textbook on life.
I'm your servant—help me understand what that means,
the inner meaning of your instructions.
It's time to act, GOD;
they've made a shambles of your revelation!
Yea-Saying God, I love what you command,
I love it better than gold and gemstones;
Yea-Saying God, I honor everything you tell me,
I despise every deceitful detour.

Every word you give me is a miracle word—
how could I help but obey?
Break open your words, let the light shine out,
let ordinary people see the meaning.

Mouth open and panting,
    I wanted your commands more than anything.
Turn my way, look kindly on me,
    as you always do to those who personally love
        you.
Steady my steps with your Word of promise
    so nothing malign gets the better of me.
Rescue me from the grip of bad men and women
    so I can live life your way.
Smile on me, your servant;
    teach me the right way to live.
I cry rivers of tears
    because nobody's living by your book!

You *are* right and you *do* right, GOD;
    your decisions are right on target.
You rightly instruct us in how to live
    ever faithful to you.
My rivals nearly did me in,
    they persistently ignored your commandments.
Your promise has been tested through and through,
    and I, your servant, love it dearly.
I'm too young to be important,
    but I don't forget what you tell me.
Your righteousness is eternally right,
    your revelation is the only truth.
Even though troubles came down on me hard,
    your commands always gave me delight.

The way you tell me to live is always right;
help me understand it so I can live to the fullest.

I call out at the top of my lungs,
"GOD! Answer! I'll do whatever you say."
I called to you, "Save me
so I can carry out all your instructions."
I was up before sunrise,
crying for help, hoping for a word from you.
I stayed awake all night,
prayerfully pondering your promise.
In your love, listen to me;
in your justice, GOD, keep me alive.
As those out to get me come closer and closer,
they go farther and farther from the truth you
reveal;
But you're the closest of all to me, GOD,
and all your judgments true.
I've known all along from the evidence of your words
that you meant them to last forever.

Take a good look at my trouble, and help me—
I haven't forgotten your revelation.
Take my side and get me out of this;
give me back my life, just as you promised.
"Salvation" is only gibberish to the wicked
because they've never looked it up in your
dictionary.

Your mercies, GOD, run into the billions;
following your guidelines, revive me.
My antagonists are too many to count,
but I don't swerve from the directions you gave.
I took one look at the quitters and was filled with loathing;
they walked away from your promises so casually!
Take note of how I love what you tell me;
out of your life of love, prolong my life.
Your words all add up to the sum total: Truth.
Your righteous decisions are eternal.

I've been slandered unmercifully by the politicians,
but my awe at your words keeps me stable.
I'm ecstatic over what you say,
like one who strikes it rich.
I hate lies—can't stand them!—
but I love what you have revealed.
Seven times each day I stop and shout praises
for the way you keep everything running right.
For those who love what you reveal, everything fits—
no stumbling around in the dark for them.
I wait expectantly for your salvation;
GOD, I do what you tell me.
My soul guards and keeps all your instructions—
oh, how much I love them!

I follow your directions, abide by your counsel;
my life's an open book before you.

Let my cry come right into your presence, GOD;
provide me with the insight that comes only
from your Word.
Give my request your personal attention,
rescue me on the terms of your promise.
Let praise cascade off my lips;
after all, you've taught me the truth about life!
And let your promises ring from my tongue;
every order you've given is right.
Put your hand out and steady me
since I've chosen to live by your counsel.
I'm homesick, GOD, for your salvation;
I love it when you show yourself!
Invigorate my soul so I can praise you well,
use your decrees to put iron in my soul.
And should I wander off like a lost sheep—seek me!
I'll recognize the sound of your voice.

120

A pilgrim song

I'm in trouble. I cry to GOD,
desperate for an answer:
"Deliver me from the liars, GOD!
They smile so sweetly but lie through their teeth."

Do you know what's next, can you see what's coming,
all you bold-faced liars?
Pointed arrows and burning coals
will be your reward.

I'm doomed to live in Meshech,
cursed with a home in Kedar,
My whole life lived camping
among quarreling neighbors.
I'm all for peace, but the minute
I tell them so, they go to war!

121

A pilgrim song

I look up to the mountains;
does my strength come from mountains?
No, my strength comes from God,
who made heaven, and earth, and mountains.

He won't let you stumble,
your Guardian God won't fall asleep.
Not on your life! Israel's
Guardian will never doze or sleep.

God's your Guardian,
right at your side to protect you—
Shielding you from sunstroke,
sheltering you from moonstroke.

GOD guards you from every evil,
    he guards your very life.
He guards you when you leave and when you
        return,
    he guards you now, he guards you always.

122

A pilgrim song of David

When they said, "Let's go to the house of GOD,"
    my heart leaped for joy.
And now we're here, oh Jerusalem,
    inside Jerusalem's walls!

Jerusalem, well-built city,
    built as a place for worship!
The city to which the tribes ascend,
    all GOD's tribes go up to worship,
To give thanks to the name of GOD—
    this is what it means to be Israel.
Thrones for righteous judgment
    are set there, famous David-thrones.

Pray for Jerusalem's peace!
    Prosperity to all you Jerusalem-lovers!
Friendly insiders, get along!
    Hostile outsiders, keep your distance!
For the sake of my family and friends,
    I say it again: live in peace!

For the sake of the house of our God, GOD,
I'll do my very best for you.

123

A pilgrim song

I look to you, heaven-dwelling God,
look up to you for help.
Like servants, alert to their master's commands,
like a maiden attending her lady,
We're watching and waiting, holding our breath,
awaiting your word of mercy.
Mercy, GOD, mercy!
We've been kicked around long enough,
Kicked in the teeth by complacent rich men,
kicked when we're down by arrogant brutes.

124

A pilgrim song of David

If GOD hadn't been for us
—all together now, Israel, sing out!—
If GOD hadn't been for us
when everyone went against us,
We would have been swallowed alive
by their violent anger,
Swept away by the flood of rage,
drowned in the torrent;
We would have lost our lives
in the wild, raging water.

Oh, blessed be GOD!
He didn't go off and leave us.
He didn't abandon us defenseless,
helpless as a rabbit in a pack of snarling dogs.

We've flown free from their fangs,
free of their traps, free as a bird.
Their grip is broken;
we're free as a bird in flight.

GOD's strong name is our help,
the same GOD who made heaven and earth.

125

A pilgrim song

Those who trust in GOD
are like Zion Mountain:
Nothing can move it, a rock-solid mountain
you can always depend on.
Mountains encircle Jerusalem,
and GOD encircles his people—
always has and always will.
The fist of the wicked
will never violate
What is due the righteous,
provoking wrongful violence.
Be good to your good people, GOD,
to those whose hearts are right!

God will round up the backsliders,
corral them with the incorrigibles.
Peace over Israel!

126

A pilgrim song

It seemed like a dream, too good to be true,
when God returned Zion's exiles.
We laughed, we sang,
we couldn't believe our good fortune.
We were the talk of the nations—
"God was wonderful to them!"
God *was* wonderful to us;
we are one happy people.

And now, God, do it again—
bring rains to our drought-stricken lives
So those who planted their crops in despair
will shout "Yes!" at the harvest,
So those who went off with heavy hearts
will come home laughing, with armloads of blessing.

127

A pilgrim song of Solomon

If God doesn't build the house,
the builders only build shacks.

If God doesn't guard the city,
  the night watchman might as well nap.
It's useless to rise early and go to bed late,
  and work your worried fingers to the bone.
Don't you know he enjoys
  giving rest to those he loves?

Don't you see that children are God's best gift?
  the fruit of the womb his generous legacy?
Like a warrior's fistful of arrows
  are the children of a vigorous youth.
Oh, how blessed are you parents,
  with your quivers full of children!
Your enemies don't stand a chance against you;
  you'll sweep them right off your doorstep.

128

A pilgrim song

All you who fear God, how blessed you are!
  how happily you walk on his smooth straight
    road!
You worked hard and deserve all you've got coming.
  Enjoy the blessing! Soak in the goodness!

Your wife will bear children as a vine bears grapes,
  your household lush as a vineyard,
The children around your table
  as fresh and promising as young olive shoots.

Stand in awe of God's Yes.
Oh, how he blesses the one who fears GOD!

Enjoy the good life in Jerusalem
every day of your life.
And enjoy your grandchildren.
Peace to Israel!

129

A pilgrim song

"They've kicked me around ever since I was young"
—this is how Israel tells it—
"They've kicked me around ever since I was young,
but they never could keep me down.
Their plowmen plowed long furrows
up and down my back;
Then GOD ripped the harnesses
of the evil plowmen to shreds."

Oh, let all those who hate Zion
grovel in humiliation;
Let them be like grass in shallow ground
that withers before the harvest,
Before the farmhands can gather it in,
the harvesters get in the crop,
Before the neighbors have a chance to call out,
"Congratulations on your wonderful crop!
We bless you in GOD's name!"

130

A pilgrim song

Help, GOD—I've hit rock bottom!
Master, hear my cry for help!
Listen hard! Open your ears!
Listen to my cries for mercy.

If you, GOD, kept records on wrongdoings,
who would stand a chance?
As it turns out, forgiveness is your habit,
and that's why you're worshiped.

I pray to GOD—my life a prayer—
and wait for what he'll say and do.
My life's on the line before God, my Lord,
waiting and watching till morning,
waiting and watching till morning.

Oh Israel, wait and watch for GOD—
with GOD's arrival comes love,
with GOD's arrival comes generous redemption.
No doubt about it—he'll redeem Israel,
buy back Israel from captivity to sin.

131

A pilgrim song

GOD, I'm not trying to rule the roost,
I don't want to be king of the mountain.

I haven't meddled where I have no business
  or fantasized grandiose plans.

I've kept my feet on the ground,
  I've cultivated a quiet heart.
Like a baby content in its mother's arms,
  my soul is a baby content.

Wait, Israel, for GOD. Wait with hope.
  Hope now; hope always!

132

A pilgrim song

O GOD, remember David,
  remember all his troubles!
And remember how he promised GOD,
  made a vow to the Strong God of Jacob,
"I'm not going home,
  and I'm not going to bed,
I'm not going to sleep,
  not even take time to rest,
Until I find a home for GOD,
  a house for the Strong God of Jacob."

Remember how we got the news in Ephrathah,
  learned all about it at Jaar Meadows?
We shouted, "Let's go to the shrine dedication!
  Let's worship at God's own footstool!"

Up, GOD, enjoy your new place of quiet repose,
you and your mighty covenant ark;
Get your priests all dressed up in justice;
prompt your worshipers to sing this prayer:
"Honor your servant David;
don't disdain your anointed one."

GOD gave David his word,
he won't back out on this promise:
"One of your sons
I will set on your throne;
If your sons stay true to my Covenant
and learn to live the way I teach them,
Their sons will continue the line—
always a son to sit on your throne.
Yes—I, GOD, chose Zion,
the place I wanted for my shrine;
This will always be my home;
this is what I want, and I'm here for good.
I'll shower blessings on the pilgrims who come here,
and give supper to those who arrive hungry;
I'll dress my priests in salvation clothes;
the holy people will sing their hearts out!
Oh, I'll make the place radiant for David!
I'll fill it with light for my anointed!
I'll dress his enemies in dirty rags,
but I'll make his crown sparkle with splendor."

133

A pilgrim song of David

How wonderful, how beautiful,
 when brothers and sisters get along!
It's like costly anointing oil
 flowing down head and beard,
Flowing down Aaron's beard,
 flowing down the collar of his priestly robes.
It's like the dew on Mount Hermon
 flowing down the slopes of Zion.
Yes, that's where GOD commands the blessing,
 ordains eternal life.

134

A pilgrim song

Come, bless GOD,
 all you servants of GOD!
You priests of GOD, posted to the nightwatch
 in GOD's shrine,
Lift your praising hands to the Holy Place,
 and bless GOD.
In turn, may GOD of Zion bless you—
 GOD who made heaven and earth!

135

Hallelujah!
Praise the name of GOD,
praise the works of GOD.
All you priests on duty in GOD's temple,
serving in the sacred halls of our God,
Shout "Hallelujah!" because GOD's so good,
sing anthems to his beautiful name.
And why? Because GOD chose Jacob,
embraced Israel as a prize possession.

I too give witness to the greatness of GOD,
our Lord, high above all other gods.
He does just as he pleases—
however, wherever, whenever.
He makes the weather—clouds and thunder,
lightning and rain, wind pouring out of the north.
He struck down the Egyptian firstborn,
both human and animal firstborn.
He made Egypt sit up and take notice,
confronted Pharaoh and his servants with miracles.
Yes, he struck down great nations,
he slew mighty kings—
Sihon king of the Amorites, also Og of Bashan—
every last one of the Canaanite kings!
Then he turned their land over to Israel,
a gift of good land to his people.

God, your name is eternal,
God, you'll never be out-of-date.
God stands up for his people,
God holds the hands of his people.
The gods of the godless nations are mere trinkets,
made for quick sale in the markets:
Chiseled mouths that can't talk,
painted eyes that can't see,
Carved ears that can't hear—
dead wood! cold metal!
Those who make and trust them
become like them.

Family of Israel, bless God!
Family of Aaron, bless God!
Family of Levi, bless God!
You who fear God, bless God!
Oh, blessed be God of Zion,
First Citizen of Jerusalem!
Hallelujah!

136

Thank God! He deserves your thanks.
His love never quits.
Thank the God of all gods,
His love never quits.
Thank the Lord of all lords.
His love never quits.

Thank the miracle-working God,
His love never quits.
The God whose skill formed the cosmos,
His love never quits.
The God who laid out earth on ocean foundations,
His love never quits.
The God who filled the skies with light,
His love never quits.
The sun to watch over the day,
His love never quits.
Moon and stars as guardians of the night,
His love never quits.
The God who struck down the Egyptian firstborn,
His love never quits.
And rescued Israel from Egypt's oppression,
His love never quits.
Took Israel in hand with his powerful hand,
His love never quits.
Split the Red Sea right in half,
His love never quits.
Led Israel right through the middle,
His love never quits.
Dumped Pharaoh and his army in the sea,
His love never quits.
The God who marched his people through the desert,
His love never quits.
Smashed huge kingdoms right and left,
His love never quits.
Struck down the famous kings,
His love never quits.

Struck Sihon the Amorite king,
His love never quits.
Struck Og the Bashanite king,
His love never quits.
Then distributed their land as booty,
His love never quits.
Handed the land over to Israel.
His love never quits.

God remembered us when we were down,
His love never quits.
Rescued us from the trampling boot,
His love never quits.
Takes care of everyone in time of need.
His love never quits.
Thank God, who did it all!
His love never quits!

137

Alongside Babylon's rivers
we sat on the banks; we cried and cried,
remembering the good old days in Zion.
Alongside the quaking aspens
we stacked our unplayed harps;
That's where our captors demanded songs,
sarcastic and mocking:
"Sing us a happy Zion song!"

Oh, how could we ever sing GOD's song
in this wasteland?

If I ever forget you, Jerusalem,
let my fingers wither and fall off like leaves.
Let my tongue swell and turn black
if I fail to remember you,
If I fail, oh dear Jerusalem,
to honor you as my greatest.

God, remember those Edomites,
and remember the ruin of Jerusalem,
That day they yelled out,
"Wreck it, smash it to bits!"
And you, Babylonians—ravagers!
A reward to whoever gets back at you
for all you've done to us;
Yes, a reward to the one who grabs your babies
and smashes their heads on the rocks!

138

A David psalm

Thank you! Everything in me says "Thank you!"
Angels listen as I sing my thanks.
I kneel in worship facing your holy temple
and say it again: "Thank you!"
Thank you for your love,
thank you for your faithfulness;
Most holy is your name,
most holy is your Word.
The moment I called out, you stepped in;
you made my life large with strength.

When they hear what you have to say, GOD,
all earth's kings will say "Thank you."
They'll sing of what you've done:
"How great the glory of GOD!"
And here's why: GOD, high above, sees far below;
no matter the distance, he knows everything
about us.

When I walk into the thick of trouble,
keep me alive in the angry turmoil.
With one hand
strike my foes,
With your other hand
save me.
Finish what you started in me, GOD.
Your love is eternal—don't quit on me now.

139

A David psalm

GOD, investigate my life;
get all the facts firsthand.
I'm an open book to you;
even from a distance, you know what I'm
thinking.
You know when I leave and when I get back;
I'm never out of your sight.
You know everything I'm going to say
before I start the first sentence.

I look behind me and you're there,
then up ahead and you're there, too—
your reassuring presence, coming and going.
This is too much, too wonderful—
I can't take it all in!

Is there anyplace I can go to avoid your Spirit?
to be out of your sight?
If I climb to the sky, you're there!
If I go underground, you're there!
If I flew on morning's wings
to the far western horizon,
You'd find me in a minute—
you're already there waiting!
Then I said to myself, "Oh, he even sees me in the dark!
At night I'm immersed in the light!"
It's a fact: darkness isn't dark to you;
night and day, darkness and light, they're all the same to you.

Oh yes, you shaped me first inside, then out;
you formed me in my mother's womb.
I thank you, High God—you're breathtaking!
Body and soul, I am marvelously made!
I worship in adoration—what a creation!
You know me inside and out,
you know every bone in my body;
You know exactly how I was made, bit by bit,
how I was sculpted from nothing into something.

Like an open book, you watched me grow from
conception to birth;
all the stages of my life were spread out before
you,
The days of my life all prepared
before I'd even lived one day.

Your thoughts—how rare, how beautiful!
God, I'll never comprehend them!
I couldn't even begin to count them—
any more than I could count the sand of the sea.
Oh, let me rise in the morning and live always
with you!
And please, God, do away with wickedness
for good!
And you murderers—out of here!—
all the men and women who belittle you, God,
infatuated with cheap god-imitations.
See how I hate those who hate you, GOD,
see how I loathe all this godless arrogance;
I hate it with pure, unadulterated hatred.
Your enemies are my enemies!

Investigate my life, O God,
find out everything about me;
Cross-examine and test me,
get a clear picture of what I'm about;
See for yourself whether I've done anything
wrong—
then guide me on the road to eternal life.

140

A David psalm

GOD, get me out of here, away from this evil;
protect me from these vicious people.
All they do is think up new ways to be bad;
they spend their days plotting war games.
They practice the sharp rhetoric of hate and hurt,
speak venomous words that maim and kill.
GOD, keep me out of the clutch of these wicked
ones,
protect me from these vicious people;
All boast and swagger, they plot ways to trip
me up,
determined to bring me down.
These crooks invent traps to catch me
and do their best to incriminate me.

I prayed, "GOD, you're my God!
Listen, GOD! Mercy!
GOD, my Lord, Strong Savior,
protect me when the fighting breaks out!
Don't let the wicked have their way, GOD,
don't give them an inch!"

These troublemakers all around me—
let them drown in their own verbal poison.
Let God pile hellfire on them,
let him bury them alive in crevasses!

These loudmouths—
    don't let them be taken seriously;
These savages—
    let the Devil hunt them down!

I know that you, GOD, are on the side of victims,
    that you care for the rights of the poor.
And I know that the righteous personally thank you,
    that good people are secure in your presence.

141

A David psalm

GOD, come close. Come quickly!
    Open your ears—it's my voice you're hearing!
Treat my prayer as sweet incense rising;
    my raised hands are my evening prayers.

Post a guard at my mouth, GOD,
    set a watch at the door of my lips.
Don't let me so much as dream of evil
    or thoughtlessly fall into bad company.
And these people who only do wrong—
    don't let them lure me with their sweet talk!
May the Just One set me straight,
    may the Kind One correct me,
Don't let sin anoint my head.
    I'm praying hard against their evil ways!
Oh, let their leaders be pushed off a high rock cliff;
    make them face the music.

Like a rock pulverized by a maul,
    let their bones be scattered at the gates of hell.

But GOD, dear Lord,
    I only have eyes for you.
Since I've run for dear life to you,
    take good care of me.
Protect me from their evil scheming,
    from all their demonic subterfuge.
Let the wicked fall flat on their faces,
    while I walk off without a scratch.

142

A David prayer—when he was in the cave

I cry out loudly to GOD,
    loudly I plead with GOD for mercy.
I spill out all my complaints before him,
    and spell out my troubles in detail:

"As I sink in despair, my spirit ebbing away,
    you know how I'm feeling,
Know the danger I'm in,
    the traps hidden in my path.
Look right, look left—
    there's not a soul who cares what happens!
I'm up against the wall, with no exit—
    it's just me, all alone.
I cry out, GOD, call out:
    'You're my last chance, my only hope for life!'

Oh listen, please listen;
    I've never been this low.
Rescue me from those who are hunting me down;
    I'm no match for them.
Get me out of this dungeon
    so I can thank you in public.
Your people will form a circle around me
    and you'll bring me showers of blessing!"

143

A David psalm

Listen to this prayer of mine, GOD;
    pay attention to what I'm asking.
Answer me—you're famous for your answers!
    Do what's right for me.
But don't, please don't, haul me into court;
    not a person alive would be acquitted there.

The enemy hunted me down;
    he kicked me and stomped me within an inch
        of my life.
He put me in a black hole,
    buried me like a corpse in that dungeon.
I sat there in despair, my spirit draining away,
    my heart heavy, like lead.
I remembered the old days,
    went over all you've done, pondered the ways
        you've worked,

Stretched out my hands to you,
as thirsty for you as a desert thirsty for rain.

Hurry with your answer, GOD!
I'm nearly at the end of my rope.
Don't turn away; don't ignore me!
That would be certain death.
If you wake me each morning with the sound of
your loving voice,
I'll go to sleep each night trusting in you.
Point out the road I must travel;
I'm all ears, all eyes before you.
Save me from my enemies, GOD—
you're my only hope!
Teach me how to live to please you,
because you're my God.
Lead me by your blessed Spirit
into cleared and level pastureland.

Keep up your reputation, GOD—give me life!
In your justice, get me out of this trouble!
In your great love, vanquish my enemies;
make a clean sweep of those who harass me.
And why? Because I'm your servant.

144

A David psalm

Blessed be GOD, my mountain,
who trains me to fight fair and well.

He's the bedrock on which I stand,
    the castle in which I live,
    my rescuing knight,
The high crag where I run for dear life,
    while he lays my enemies low.

I wonder why you care, GOD—
    why do you bother with us at all?
All we are is a puff of air;
    we're like shadows in a campfire.

Step down out of heaven, GOD;
    ignite volcanoes in the hearts of the mountains.
Hurl your lightnings in every direction;
    shoot your arrows this way and that.
Reach all the way from sky to sea:
    pull me out of the ocean of hate,
    out of the grip of those barbarians
Who lie through their teeth,
    who shake your hand
    then knife you in the back.

O God, let me sing a new song to you,
    let me play it on a twelve-string guitar—
A song to the God who saved the king,
    the God who rescued David, his servant.

Rescue me from the enemy sword,
    release me from the grip of those barbarians
Who lie through their teeth,

who shake your hand
then knife you in the back.

Make our sons in their prime
like sturdy oak trees,
Our daughters as shapely and bright
as fields of wildflowers.
Fill our barns with great harvest,
fill our fields with huge flocks;
Protect us from invasion and exile—
eliminate the crime in our streets.

How blessed the people who have all this!
How blessed the people who have God for God!

145

David's praise

I lift you high in praise, my God, O my King!
and I'll bless your name into eternity.

I'll bless you every day,
and keep it up from now to eternity.

God is magnificent; he can never be praised
enough.
There are no boundaries to his greatness.

Generation after generation stands in awe of your
work;
each one tells stories of your mighty acts.

Your beauty and splendor have everyone talking;
    I compose songs on your wonders.

Your marvelous doings are headline news;
    I could write a book full of the details of your
        greatness.

The fame of your goodness spreads across the
        country;
    your righteousness is on everyone's lips.

GOD is all mercy and grace—
    not quick to anger, is rich in love.

GOD is good to one and all;
    everything he does is soaked through with grace.

Creation and creatures applaud you, GOD;
    your holy people bless you.

They talk about the glories of your rule,
    they exclaim over your splendor,

Letting the world know of your power for good,
    the lavish splendor of your kingdom.

Your kingdom is a kingdom eternal;
    you never get voted out of office.

GOD always does what he says,
    and is gracious in everything he does.

God gives a hand to those down on their luck,
gives a fresh start to those ready to quit.

All eyes are on you, expectant;
you give them their meals on time.

Generous to a fault,
you lavish your favor on all creatures.

Everything God does is right—
the trademark on all his works is love.

God's there, listening for all who pray,
for all who pray and mean it.

He does what's best for those who fear him—
hears them call out, and saves them.

God sticks by all who love him,
but it's all over for those who don't.

My mouth is filled with God's praise.
Let everything living bless him,
bless his holy name from now to eternity!

146

Hallelujah!
Oh my soul, praise God!
All my life long I'll praise God,
singing songs to my God as long as I live.

Don't put your life in the hands of experts
    who know nothing of life, of *salvation* life.
Mere humans don't have what it takes;
    when they die, their projects die with them.
Instead, get help from the God of Jacob,
    put your hope in GOD and know real blessing!
GOD made sky and soil,
    sea and all the fish in it.
He always does what he says—
    he defends the wronged,
    he feeds the hungry.
GOD frees prisoners—
    he gives sight to the blind,
    he lifts up the fallen.
GOD loves good people, protects strangers,
    takes the side of orphans and widows,
    but makes short work of the wicked.

GOD's in charge—*always*.
    Zion's God is God for good!
    Hallelujah!

147

Hallelujah!
It's a good thing to sing praise to our God;
    praise is beautiful, praise is fitting.

GOD's the one who rebuilds Jerusalem,
    who regathers Israel's scattered exiles.

He heals the heartbroken
    and bandages their wounds.
He counts the stars
    and assigns each a name.
Our Lord is great, with limitless strength;
    we'll never comprehend what he knows and does.
GOD puts the fallen on their feet again
    and pushes the wicked into the ditch.

Sing to GOD a thanksgiving hymn,
    play music on your instruments to God,
Who fills the sky with clouds,
    preparing rain for the earth,
Then turning the mountains green with grass,
    feeding both cattle and crows.
He's not impressed with horsepower;
    the size of our muscles means little to him.
Those who fear GOD get GOD's attention;
    they can depend on his strength.

Jerusalem, worship GOD!
    Zion, praise your God!
He made your city secure,
    he blessed your children among you.
He keeps the peace at your borders,
    he puts the best bread on your tables.
He launches his promises earthward—
    how swift and sure they come!
He spreads snow like a white fleece,
    he scatters frost like ashes,

He broadcasts hail like birdseed—
    who can survive his winter?
Then he gives the command and it all melts;
    he breathes on winter—suddenly it's spring!

He speaks the same way to Jacob,
    speaks words that work to Israel.
He never did this to the other nations;
    they never heard such commands.
Hallelujah!

148

Hallelujah!
Praise GOD from heaven,
    praise him from the mountaintops;
Praise him, all you his angels,
    praise him, all you his warriors,
Praise him, sun and moon,
    praise him, you morning stars;
Praise him, high heaven,
    praise him, heavenly rain clouds;
Praise, oh let them praise the name of GOD—
    he spoke the word, and there they were!

He set them in place
    from all time to eternity;
He gave his orders,
    and that's it!

Praise GOD from earth,
    you sea dragons, you fathomless ocean deeps;
Fire and hail, snow and ice,
    hurricanes obeying his orders;
Mountains and all hills,
    apple orchards and cedar forests;
Wild beasts and herds of cattle,
    snakes, and birds in flight;
Earth's kings and all races,
    leaders and important people,
Robust men and women in their prime,
    and yes, graybeards and little children.

Let them praise the name of GOD—
    it's the only Name worth praising.
His radiance exceeds anything in earth and sky;
    he's built a monument—his very own people!

Praise from all who love GOD!
    Israel's children, intimate friends of GOD.
Hallelujah!

149

Hallelujah!
Sing to GOD a brand-new song,
    praise him in the company of all who love him.
Let all Israel celebrate their Sovereign Creator,
    Zion's children exult in their King.

Let them praise his name in dance;
strike up the band and make great music!
And why? Because GOD delights in his people,
adorns plain folk with salvation garlands!

Let true lovers break out in praise,
sing out from wherever they're sitting,
Shout the high praises of God,
brandish their swords in the wild sword-dance—
A portent of vengeance on the God-defying nations,
a signal that punishment's coming,
Their kings chained and hauled off to jail,
their leaders behind bars for good,
The judgment on them carried out to the letter
—and all who love God in the seat of honor!
Hallelujah!

150

Hallelujah!
Praise God in his holy house of worship,
praise him under the open skies;
Praise him for his acts of power,
praise him for his magnificent greatness;
Praise with a blast on the trumpet,
praise by strumming soft strings;
Praise him with castanets and dance,
praise him with banjo and flute;

Praise him with cymbals and a big bass drum,
    praise him with fiddles and mandolin.
Let every living, breathing creature praise GOD!
    Hallelujah!

ABOUT THE AUTHOR

EUGENE H. PETERSON is a writer, poet, and retired pastor. He has authored more than thirty-four books (not including *The Message*). He is Professor Emeritus of Spiritual Theology at Regent College in Vancouver, British Columbia. Eugene also founded Christ Our King Presbyterian Church in Bel Air, Maryland, where he ministered for twenty-nine years. After teaching at a seminary, he created *The Message*, a vibrant Bible translation that connects with today's readers like no other.

The Message took Peterson ten years to complete. He worked not from any English text but from the original Hebrew and Greek texts to guarantee authenticity. At the same time, his ear was always tuned to the cadence and energy of the English spoken every day on the streets. He lives with his wife, Jan, in Montana.